MORE *Faith Stories* FROM WOMEN IN THE PEWS

More Faith Stories from Women in the Pews

ISBN 978-1-7644905-0-4

The stories in this collection have been compiled and edited by Jennifer Lang. The stories are those of the women who contributed them, and Jennifer takes no responsibility for matters of fact or inference.

Enquiries about this publication may be directed to:
Jennifer Lang
Tuggeranong Uniting Church
PO Box 423
Erindale Centre ACT 2903
connections@tuc.org.au

Cover and book design: Bill Lang

A catalogue record for this book is available from the National Library of Australia

TABLE OF CONTENTS

FOREWORD

The stories gathered here and in the previous publication *Faith Stories from Women in the Pews*, are not polished success stories or spiritual highlight reels. They are honest accounts of lives shaped by faith over time. Some are dramatic, marked by clear moments of calling, rescue, or transformation. Others are quieter, unfolding in our community, our homes and churches. Yet all of them bear witness to the same truth: God is faithful, present, and deeply involved in the lives of His people.

You may find yourself reflected in these pages where you recognise your own questions, your own longings, or your own quiet faithfulness. You may have wondered whether your life is significant, whether your gifts are too small, your story too ordinary, or your obedience too hidden. This book affirms that yes, God is at work in you too.

These faith stories may encourage you to listen more closely for God's voice in your own life and remind you that no story is insignificant when placed in His hands. May you come away with renewed confidence that God who has been faithful to these women is faithful still: working, calling, and moving in ways both ordinary and extraordinary.

It has brought immense pleasure to partner with Jenny to bring this book to fruition, including making a modest contribution with the book design, and also to pen a foreword, reflecting on how these collected stories may shine a light into our own stories.

Bill Lang

INTRODUCTION

This is the second book of collected faith stories from women in the pews. I had thought the first edition was a life's work, God's work was not finished yet! Book 1 was very much prompted by COVID times and our gratefulness for physical reconnection with other people. How amazing and miraculous it is that book 2 came about within 3 years with another 20 stories! Now there are 41 stories across the two books. In these stories about our faith journeys, we see a powerful narrative of faith, hope, grace, courage and resilience. Be blessed in reading them all and discover the rich tapestry of God's enduring presence in our lives. They are all very different, as we are and vary in length and style. They also cover a diverse range of experiences both denominational and expressions of Christianity. There lies the richness of our faith journeys as we travel the path with Jesus.

Many of the stories were shared at our Church Women's Breakfast times, some recently and others some time ago. Some have more of a talk feel to them particularly, if transcribed later from a recording. Others have been specifically written to be included in the book. Some are about the church in action and some very personal. Some may challenge your Christian perspective. One is from a resource "Illness, Recovery and Wellbeing", written by a work colleague several years ago following her own experience with breast cancer. Writing the resource moved her therapeutically to write her own spirituality story as the last chapter and which she has so graciously allowed to be include. Many thanks to my friend Margaret M who kept me to the Book 2 idea once I mentioned it could be. Thankyou to my amazing contributors and to my husband Bill for bringing it to completion and getting it printed.

I trust these differing ordinary and extraordinary stories will be an encouragement to you and something you can share with friends and family. Let me encourage you to share your story, to sow the seeds of God's love, justice and compassion in our neighbourhood and beyond. Let the light of Christ shine through each of us as we bloom where we are planted and journey through our Christian lives.

As the prophet Micah asked his congregation, may we be similarly challenged: "What does the Lord require of you? And may our response be similarly, to act justly and to love mercy and walk humbly with our God."

Blessings

Jenny Lang

1

STORIES MATTER

What is your story?
Stories matter. Your story matters because YOU matter.

My name is Margaret and for many years I have been writing stories. In April it will be fifty years since my first book was published. I've always loved reading stories and often my favourite books are biographies, where the writer is trying to capture the life and experience of a real person, with all their challenges and ups and downs, or stories set in a particular time and place in history.

In thinking about the stories I have written, it occurs to me that there is a pattern. Almost all the stories are about people who were not able to write their own, or had been almost invisible and so would never have expected anyone to be interested. Mostly with women as the main characters.

People ask me, 'What led you to writing in the first place?' My mother wrote short stories and three books for young adults so in our home, writing was a normal thing to do. I always loved the process of making up stories, from childhood. In my early twenties I went to work as a teacher and then Christian Education worker in the Highlands of PNG in 1961 and was fascinated by what I was seeing there. Against what seemed a very exotic background, I was watching the very first beginnings of a Christian community in a place that had only seen their first white face, their first wheel and their first piece of paper ten years before I arrived there. When I tentatively suggested to my colleagues that I would love to try to write about it, there was not overwhelming encouragement, but I tend to be a bit pig-headed when I get an idea and I made a start on it in 1968. I found that I loved the process of researching a story and then writing it.

If ever you think that you would like to write, either your own story or someone else's, there are some key questions to consider.

Who is this for? Your own family, or a particular group who might be interested? Maybe you would like to tell your own story in a private journal, for your eyes only, as a way to reflecting on your life.

Is this your story to tell? If it is someone else's story, would they prefer to tell it in their own way. Or for you to keep out of it? Or to keep them out of your story. Be careful. Just because someone's personal story is dramatic or weird, it can turn into gossip in someone else's voice. Ask permission. Example: *Noreen's story, No Fixed Address*. She asked me to do it, and I checked everything with her.

Is this story as accurate as possible? We will all have own perspective and memories and that is natural. In telling any story, our own or someone else's, you will be selecting which parts to include and what to leave out. I find that even when I really try to make the story as truthful as I can, someone will not be happy. Example: *Whereabouts Unknown* and angry letters from woman who thought that I was promoting a deluded fable about the loss of the ship Montevideo Maru.

How do I find out the information for my books? For the books set in the past, through research. Libraries, in public and church archive collections, in old newspapers. For *Pacific Missionary*, there were enormous amounts of personal letters, journals, photographs and published material held in major libraries as well as private material and objects held by family members. For *Whereabouts Unknown* and *A Very Long War*, a combination of interviews with survivors and exploring wartime documentation in the AWM and National Archives. For *Certain Lives*, many interviews with family members as well as searching through local histories and old newspapers. For *Live Peace*, many long interviews and discussions with the key person, as well as church records and published material in church magazines. Where possible, I love to travel to see places that have been part of the story. That helps to imagine and then write a scene.

Is this fact or fiction? It can be a tricky business trying to include imagination into a story from the past where you have some hard evidence but are trying to interpret and bring it to life. Example: *Currency Lass*. I had been able to read personal letters and diaries of the key people in this story but decided to write the story as if Mary, the main character, was telling her own story. Did Mary really cry and demand answers from God when her first baby died days after her father during a flu epidemic? When I stood in the old cemetery in Parramatta and looked at the tombstone for her father and baby, I felt sure that she did. I was a bit disappointed when the National Library listed this book as fiction, as I could cite evidence for almost every event or attitude, but they told me, "You included dialogue so it is fiction."

Is it possible to have a book published these days? Many things have changed since I began writing. Technology has certainly changed. In the past, I was able to give my manuscript to a publisher, who would decide whether to publish or not, and then I would work with an editor and a book designer who did everything until you had a finished printed book. Then they did the marketing and I received royalties. No more! You need to be famous or very fortunate to find a traditional publisher. For *George Brown* it was produced as an eBook by a university press, so they supported preparation of the book but there were no royalties. For *Live Peace*, I had the support of an editor and book designer and printer, but I had to fundraise to pay them for the privilege. These days with computer programs it is possible to prepare your own work ready to be printed, so self-publishing is possible, but it costs. Our most recent book was self-published, with the help of an excellent book designer.

Sometimes people said, "You should write your own story." It always seemed a bit pretentious to consider. Then there came a time when I thought, 'Why not? Something for our grandchildren.' Both my husband Ron and I were in our 80s and his health was failing. If we were ever going to record our own experience, we needed to get on with it. We agreed that the story was a shared one and had to include the way in which our long courtship had unfolded.

One day early in 2020 we talked about some key moments that we wanted to include and I made some rough notes. Two weeks later COVID arrived in full force in Australia and everything went into lockdown. Suddenly all our usual activities stopped and, like everyone else, we stayed at home. Although we certainly had not planned or expected it, this writing project turned out to be the perfect thing to keep us interested and occupied. We had lots of old letters that we had written to each other before we were married, when I was working in Papua New Guinea and Ron was studying and working in Sydney. There were letters I had written to my parents and whole files of documents each of us had saved related to family, work and travel. There were albums of photos and our own memories. We had many long conversations, recalling things we had experienced. Ron told me more detail about his mother who died when he was only thirteen and shared some stories I had never heard. It was my role to do the actual writing, but we shared all the memories and Ron read and edited the chapters. We agreed that we had lived a very rich life together. We jokingly called this project our *Magnum Opus*, our great work, and our family referred to it as *The Opus*.

We came to the point early in 2021 when I had written a first draft up to the present day. It was not clear how to finish the story, so we decided to start again at Chapter 1 and start revising and correcting - and shortening! Ron was already corresponding with a potential publisher. One Monday in August we completed the revisions on Chapter 10. That night Ron became very ill and was taken to hospital. A week later he died. During that very hard week, with Canberra in lockdown and only being able to be with Ron in hospital when the doctors knew that he was dying, I tried to occupy myself by revising a chapter and found myself staring at words written to describe our wedding day, when we made vows to each other to be faithful "until death do us part." One of his final instructions to me was that he wanted me to finish our story. It became my personal journey in grief, to work each day on the story of a life we had shared and, with the help of my family, to arrange for images, cover design and printing.

About the cover design. For quite some time, Ron had said that it would be good to take a photo of us holding hands to go on the cover. We held hands a lot. We tried, with all sorts of angles, but were never satisfied that we had the right image. On his very last day with us, our daughter Jenni said, 'Let me try again' and one of those images is on the cover. In the week when Ron was in hospital, Jenni brought a piece of her own art to our son David's home and it became a special focus with candles and photos of Ron with his grandchildren over the next weeks. Now it forms part of the cover design so has personal meaning for our family.

Not everyone will choose, or even want, to write a whole book about their life. But I encourage you to respect your own story and find a way to tell it. Perhaps it will be a story told to a friend, as an encouragement, of some personal experience that has been important to you. Perhaps there may be a time when you can share part of your own story, with your church congregation, telling ways in which you have met God. Some of my friends have chosen a selection of photos to create a photo book for their children and grandchildren. One friend tells me that he is writing his memoir, not as a tale of triumph but of a lot of grief and regret; he told me that he hoped that this would help his family who are estranged from him to understand who he is, and why his life has turned out the way it has. Two friends have told me about an app (eg memowrite), where they are given a series of leading questions which they answer each week, recalling and recording parts of their lives as a gift for their family. When finished it is sent off electronically and returns to you as a book. I have heard that one of the gifts of time being offered at the hospice at Clare Holland House is that people will sit with someone to record some important things about their life; this is a respectful act of seeing that person as a unique human being whose life has mattered.

I believe that everyone's story does matter with both the light and the shadows.

Some of the books I have written

R + M: a love story	Margaret and Ron's story is an inspiring account of their loving partnership in life and ministry over more than 50 years. Their courage and willingness to carefully discern the Spirit's leading, ensures in remarkable adventures. The story is told with warmth, humour and humility.
Torn Between Two Worlds	Two men in PNG Highlands. One of them illiterate. Observing first contact and the growth of a young church.
Currency Lass	a young woman, not famous, married to a man who features in church history books. Went to Tonga as a missionary couple in 1822 from Sydney.
Certain Lives	an ordinary family with a very typical story of migration, early struggles to settle, gold rush, building and losing a business, drought, flood, war, Depression
No Fixed Address	a woman who worked with homeless people for 40 years, and their stories
Whereabouts Unknown	Families and single women linked with Methodist Mission who were impacted by the fall of Rabaul to the Japanese in 1942 and who spent the next three and a half years not knowing whether their men lived or were dead. These families believed that no one knew or cared about their loss.

A Singular Woman The daughter of a well-known man, who was one of the first women to graduate from University of Sydney

2

CALLED TO CURATE

Here's a little bit of my story. My name is Amanda, and I grew up in the Uniting Church. I was born ten years after the union of the Congregational, Methodist and Presbyterian churches. Union was 1977 so I did not know the other denominations before the Uniting Church formed. I would say that I'm a true Uniting Church baby.

I grew up going to my local Uniting Church in Western Sydney. My parents started going there, because they started taking me to a playgroup. It was a secular playgroup, but there were people there who were part of the church. They came along every week to connect with the parents and carers. They kept asking my parents when they were going to come to church. My parents got so annoyed at the fact that these people were asking them when they're coming to church, that they finally caved in, and they came, and they've never left.

I started coming to church when I was three years old, going to Sunday school, playing with my friends at the back of the church, because church was really boring, and I didn't want to be there. For my mum, church was about community and for my dad, his faith was kind of a hodgepodge of new age spiritualism, Buddhism, and a little bit of Christianity, all thrown in together. He didn't mind going along to the local uniting church. When I was around 12 years old, Sunday school felt a little bit too young for me. I didn't want to do any more colouring in of pictures. We had two members of our church, Chris and Sirica, who started a youth group. It was a Friday night youth group with your typical youth group games and fun. On Sunday, we had Salsa (called that because one of us couldn't open a salsa jar) but then became SOS, Salsa on Sunday.

At Salsa on Sunday, we spoke about theological concepts. When I was 12 years old, we were discussing what is grace, and what is mercy, and who is God anyway, and what's the difference between God and Jesus and the Holy Spirit.

A few years later a new minister come to our church. There was a young cohort in my congregation, and he encouraged us to be part of the band. My friends and I became the Sunday worship band. It was interesting! I don't know about the quality of the music, but we were encouraged to be part of the church service. That was a huge part of my faith formation, being respected as a young person within the church, being respected as someone who could contribute to worship in meaningful ways. A few years passed, our youth group was still going, and then, Chris and Sarika, who were our youth group leaders told us that Chris was off to start studying theology at the United Theological College, so they had to leave the congregation, which was very, very sad.

Our thought was, well, who's going to lead the youth group? Now, I was about 16 at the time, and no one was stepping up. I looked at my friends, and said, Well, why don't we do it? My younger sister had her little group of friends, and so we started a youth group for that younger age group. It grew and became a Friday night youth group. Where I grew up was a low socioeconomic part of Western Sydney. The youth group became huge because Friday night was either spent making your own fun on the streets, or you came to youth group and went bowling and other fun things, with 20 to 50 kids. During that time, I was going to the Uniting Church in the morning, but being in my later teens, I began to explore other churches in the evening for two reasons. Firstly, as I was still in the worship band I didn't feel I was getting a lot out of the morning worship services aside from me contributing to the music. Secondly, I wanted to explore what else was out there, probably because there were no guys in our congregation, and there were potentially other guys to date at other evening churches. I didn't find anyone. I tried out an evangelical Baptist church, and would regularly go to Hillsong, which is in Baulkham Hills, near where I used to live. For a few more years that would be my pattern. I would go to the

Uniting Church in the morning, I would go to Hillsong at night, ever looking for my new boyfriend, and I would be running the Uniting Church youth group as a volunteer on a Friday night.

I finished high school with a love of art. My plan in my late years of high school was to study art history and theory, because I wanted to be a curator. I loved the idea of exploring a place and a space where people could love art as much as I do. I loved the idea of taking people on a journey through an exhibition and understanding the whys and the wherefores, and noting, "have you noticed that this particular artist uses a lot of green, that's because this happened in their past. That's the colour that they relate to," and opening people's eyes and hearts and minds up to it.

I was a very high achieving perfectionist and became exhausted and burnt out. After my HSC I took a gap year, doing a bit of work in retail at Millers. Then I landed a job at an art store, which I just absolutely loved. I would work in the art world through the week, and I would work in the church on the weekends. I enjoyed what I did in the art store, putting together the student packs for what they needed when they started their university courses in fashion design, or visual arts, or engineering, or architecture. But I really, really enjoyed planning and running youth groups on a Friday night as a volunteer.

I probably put too much time into planning those youth group nights and when it was time for me to take up my university offer after my gap year, something didn't feel right. I put it down to just continuing to recover from my burnout. I rescinded the university offer and thought if I want to go back to it, I can later. But right then, I needed to figure out what was next.

My parents were putting pressure on me as well, because I wasn't going to university and I was working. My father was university educated so he wanted me to have a university education too. But at that point, I was delving deeper into my faith and theology. I had a lot of spare time on my hands and was living with my parents. I had a thirst for learning more about faith and theology. I would toddle off to Koorong, the local Christian bookshop near me. I would pull books off the shelves and read the blurbs and buy the ones that I thought would suit me and my life. And I would read. I would read the Bible, in the way that I was taught as a child, which was just reading the Bible and seeing what you get out of it.

I did find someone to date during that time, and he introduced me to a book called *Velvet Elvis* by Rob Bell. That began to shift my theology. Sadly, or not sadly, we broke up, and I found a better guy, David. Midway through my second gap year, I have a distinct memory of sitting in my bed, one evening and just stressing about not being able to figure out what I wanted to do with myself. It wasn't a voice that came to me, it was a feeling that came to me, and I don't know how to better describe it. And that feeling said to me, why not do what you love doing, which is youth group? This was a light bulb moment for me.

The next day, I marched myself out of my bedroom, made some breakfast, and came into my parents' room, and told them "I know what I want to study, and its youth ministry." My mum went, "oh no" because there was a slight issue. I had a major phobia of public speaking. A major, major phobia. Through primary school, I would have panic attacks about public speaking. Throughout high school, I would have panic attacks about public speaking to the point that my parents took me to drama school to try and help the situation. How on earth was I going to do ministry if I couldn't do public speaking?

The next week, my minister had heard that I was interested in studying youth ministry and ministry and he gave me the preaching slot on a Sunday morning. I really enjoyed putting a sermon together. I wouldn't call it a sermon these days. But I put something together, I think it was about Ephesians, and I was nervous. I had all of the symptoms that I would normally have with my public speaking phobia: sweaty palms, shaking knees, the feeling of wanting to throw up, which I did, by the way, though not that Sunday. I thought, Oh gosh, maybe this is wrong, maybe this call isn't right, maybe youth ministry isn't the thing. I remember walking up to the pulpit, putting my piece of paper down that had my sermon on it, and I preached. It was the first time that I had ever felt still and settled within myself. It was the first time that I'd ever public spoke and didn't need to run off into a back room and hyperventilate. It was the first time that I got excited about speaking into a microphone.

When I got home that evening, having been at the Uniting Church in the morning and Hillsong at night, I found on my bed a list of courses in youth ministry that my mum had printed off and left for me. A few days later I had dinner with Chris and Sureka, who were my youth group leaders. They'd become my mentors and I often had dinner at their place on a Wednesday night. Chris was now an ordained minister in the Uniting Church, and I told them I wanted to check something with them and that I knew what I was meant to be doing. When I told them I need to be studying youth ministry there response was "Thank goodness." Sureka left the table and returned with *Faith Seeking Understanding*, an introductory textbook at United Theological College. "We bought this for you two years ago. Take it and I'll drive you tomorrow to get registered."

The next day, I was enrolled into a diploma of youth ministry at United Theological College. In February 2008 I began that journey and it was a tough journey. I had to do group presentations, and I wasn't completely cured of my phobia, but when you're studying theology, you are broken apart to put you back together again. My understanding of God, faith, Jesus, spirit, grace, and forgiveness were torn down, because I was learning so much about biblical context. I was learning about the nuances of faith and apologetics. Why do good things happen to bad people and why do bad things happen to good people?

I was 19 and most of my cohort were at least thirty to forty years older. I finished my diploma in youth ministry. During that time I stopped going to Hillsong at night. I had nothing against Hillsong but it didn't match who I was anymore or how I wanted to worship.

The minister at Wahroonga Uniting Church in Sydney contacted me about a part-time Children, Youth and Family position coming up. I got the position and I learned a lot about children's ministry during that time. I cut my teeth, so to speak, in congregational work, realising that the church isn't as rosy as we make it out to be, and that we're just a bunch of messy people who come together to worship a God who loves us in our messiness. I finished my diploma and then immediately enrolled in a Bachelor of Theology, because the high achieving perfectionist was going to be the best gosh darn youth pastor you've ever seen. I'm going to be so equipped. I'm going to make sure that I know everything there is to know about theology. Well, as it turns out, the more you study theology, the more you realise you don't know anything about anything. The diploma of youth ministry opened my mind up to the world of theology and philosophy, and I was thirsty for that knowledge.

I got some more part time work doing a stint at Parramatta-Nepean Presbytery as their office admin person. This is where I met David, but only over the phone. David was the secretary of Sydney Presbytery at the time, and so he would often call me up to ask do you have x, y, z? I wasn't really cut out for office work, so I got a job as well with the Sydney North and Kuringai Youth Project, (SNAK) resourcing other children, youth, and family pastors in the area.

The high achieving perfectionist in me wanted all the tools. So I got another job as well with too many jobs ending in burnout. I blame my youth and I took a bit of a break. I decided that I couldn't work multiple part time jobs because that equalled multiple full-time jobs. You can't leave ministry, unfortunately. It's not a nine to five role. You take it with you everywhere. I'd been in and out of home at that point when a position came up for a residential assistant at Burwood Student House as a part of Burwood Uniting Church. They had a big tertiary community there, and they wanted a mother hen to come and live in there and create intentional Christian community with the students who were also living in the house. It was an interesting experiment. I did a year there, and it was it was hard yakka. I was doing tertiary ministry at the time, so I was expanding from children and youth and family to now tertiary ministry. I loved doing tertiary ministry. I found out that many of the students who came to live in the house didn't want an intentional Christian community. They just said that on their form as they just wanted a cheap place to live. I felt like I couldn't do my job correctly, and so I moved out of the student house. That year was really formative as it taught me what it meant to live in an intentional Christian community. It also gave me an opportunity to do some resource ministry for the Burwood Evening Congregation.

The Burwood Evening Congregation was an interesting mix of tertiary students and people who were rough sleepers. The church was on the main strip of Burwood in between the Westfield and the train station. We would offer meals on a Sunday night, usually for the hungry students. But what ended up happening was that people would hear that there was a free meal and those who were living out on the streets, or who were suffering from schizophrenia, or who had any sort of need at all, would come into the church space knowing that they had a safe and warm place to be for two hours on a Sunday night. I also did a lot of ministry with people on the streets and it was just so fulfilling to be able to be a person who could help in that way.

That was the year I also ran back into David. We ran EURORA which was the National Christian Youth Convention, in North Parramatta. I'd never been to one before, so I thought, well, as high achieving perfectionist, surely I can organise one. I ran program, and we got David in to do the Geeky Stuff. David was in charge of all the walkie talkies and communications, and that's how our friendship and eventually relationship began. That was a big year.

As I moved from doing children, youth and family ministry, to tertiary ministry to ministry with those on the streets, to resourcing a congregation, my phobia of public speaking stopped, which was good. I realised more and more that I was feeling a calling to serve the church in a bigger way for a wider audience, not just children and youth and family, not just tertiary, not just people who need our help, but also just everyone. I started a period of discernment, as it's called in the Uniting Church, because I wanted to figure out what to do.

I didn't want to just be a children's pastor. I didn't want to just be a tertiary minister. But I did not want to be an ordained minister. No chance whatsoever. I didn't look like a minister. I didn't act like a minister. I was not going to don a pair of sandals and wear an alb. I just wasn't going to do it.

I started a period of discernment and my mentor was the Reverend Aimee Kent. At my first meeting with Aimee, I sat her down and said, "I am called to ministry in the Uniting Church. It is a lifelong call to ministry in the Uniting Church. It is a call to serve everyone in the Uniting Church, and there is no way in hell I'm going to become a minister." We explored different options, and whether God was actually calling me, and I wasn't listening. She dropped what I would call a lot of truth bombs at that point. She held up a mirror and helped me see that perhaps God was calling me into ordained ministry because of who I was and not in spite of it.

God was calling me into ordained ministry because I wanted to curate space for people. God was calling me into ordained ministry because of who I am and not in spite of it. During my period of discernment, I was having conversations with many ministers. A dear friend, a minister said, "Amanda, if you can do any other job, do it." I remember replying, "I don't think I can. I don't think I can deny this call." She said, "then you're called to ministry." I got home blubbering to David saying "I think I'm called to be ordained" and he said yes, "I told you on our first date that I wanted to become a minister's wife."

David got what he always dreamed. I enrolled in my Master's course because I'm a high achieving perfectionist. We got engaged and I started the formation process. Through formation, I continued to work at Burwood, and it was thought I might be good at school chaplaincy, so I did some work at MLC Burwood and Pymble Ladies College. I then went to Balmain Uniting Church in my last placement.

My first ordained placement and call was to Berowra Uniting Church. I realised that I had become a curator. I'd become what I wanted to be and more. I see my role in ministry as creating a space for people to experience God and faith and to maybe see what I see, to take people on a journey, to allow them to play and explore. My pathway continues and it hasn't stopped. It will never stop. But I know that in the end, I'm called because of who I am and not in spite of it. And I'm called to curate - just in a different way.

3

LIFE'S TRANSITIONS

My name is Andi and I've been pondering and thinking about what to write for my story so I will start at the beginning. I was born here in Canberra and the oldest of two boys. I had a younger brother who died of liver cancer almost three years ago. My family has been in the Canberra region for five generations. I have relatives all throughout this area though a very small immediate family with my parents and myself. I have an aunt who now lives in Sydney and an uncle and aunt living in Queensland and a few cousins. My more distant family is all throughout Southeast Australia and around Australia as well.

When I was 20 months old, an important event of my life happened. I got very sick with gastroenteritis. I ended up in hospital for three weeks, most of the time in intensive care, in fact, in isolation intensive care. I had three cardiac arrests, and they brought me back but with brain damage. This event still is part of me today. I had to learn everything again.

I remember a story my parents told me once about one of my grandmothers went screaming down the down the hall after I got myself up. I was always one, who never seemed to be in a hurry for things, but I had started walking again, and for her I was always my family's miracle. I was not meant to be here. I always had to play catch up at school and still play catch up today. I have realised recently that I'm actually a disabled person. I have acquired brain injury, that I've lived with all my life.

My accent is not all Aussie, that's because just before my third birthday, when I was still relearning things and still starting to learn to talk, my family went to live in London for three years. I came back with a beautiful South London English accent, and everybody thought I was a pom for a few years till I picked up the Australian one again.

I have always found it difficult to make friends. I'm transgender. I knew this even as a child, and I thought I'm nuts, I'm crazy. I'm ashamed. I was always quiet, a good listener, very small and liked feminine things. So here am I, in the nineteen seventies Australia, very macho and misogynistic. Boys don't cry, boys are good at sport. I was never good at sport. I hated sport, being impacted by my brain injury, and I'm also a bit dyslexic.

In school, I was this quiet one, very feminine and every time I'd make try to make friends, mostly with boys, they turned into my worst enemies. They bullied me. I was bullied terribly throughout my childhood from about year two through to about year nine. I repeated year nine because of my brain injury. I had a very quiet, isolated, lonely childhood.

I remember watching a YouTube one day about a trans lady who had done a lot of education with people who are transgender to businesses and other people. She was saying, people like me who are trans and we know we're transgender, trans feminine, in my case, get very good at appearing how the world wants us to appear. I was born male.

Relationships have been interesting for me because I am not good at contacting people. I consider myself a terrible friend. I got it in my crazy brain here that I'm just going to put people off. Why don't they want to talk to me? I think it's come from the effect of the bullies in my life. I still fight with this today. I do apologise if I don't contact people, but you are still my friends, and I still rely on you.

I grew up in the Church of England and I was baptised as a small child but I grew up without faith. My parents didn't go to church. I didn't go to church. My family doesn't go to church. It is interesting to see me today, a person with faith, strong faith in Christ.

I was very average at school. They didn't know then that I was dyslexic, but my mum arranged a remedial class for me when I was in primary school. I still remember before dinner every night, dad would get me before we ate to go through the spelling lists and learn the time times table. Dad knew he had a son with those issues, and it took a while to learn things. Once I learnt things, it usually stuck in my head, but it takes a while sometimes. I finished school and l didn't know what to do. I did the exam for the public service and was facing unemployment.

At the time, I did square dancing. I was a good square dancer, advanced level square dancing. Through the square dancing, a couple of women friends of mine, invited me to a youth camp, at Birragai, just outside of Canberra, in January 1983. It was organised by the Catholic Charismatics, now I'm Anglican at the time. I went and met Jesus Christ and changed my life. Jesus loves me as I am. I didn't like me as I am. I thought to be loved, I had to be perfect, and I wasn't, and I couldn't be. But I tried my darndest to be perfect. The camp went for a week and as I was an Anglican and not a Catholic after the camp, decided to check out what the Anglican church had to offer. I went and knocked on the door of the local Anglican church.

I was living in Weston Creek area where I grew up and got involved with three Anglican parishes in Weston Creek and for many years was involved in a youth program called Camp Pelican. At first I was one of their bus drivers, then helping out in the kitchen and eventually as one of the counsellors. I was still trying to figure out what to do with my life, and what is this faith?

Where, what am I to do with my life? I kept asking God, and God is, God does, He/she is very slow. I needed to do a lot of healing. I eventually joined the public service working for the Royal Canberra Hospital, an internal courier, and then in medical records, but still trying to figure out what to do with my life.

I thought about religious life for a while. I remember seeing, Anthony Hopkins' TV program about Saint Paul and thinking, I'd love to have that faith one day, do what Saint Paul did, go and announce the gospel, announce this relationship that was still growing with me with God trying to pull me out of my isolation and my loneliness and my shyness. I used to go into meetings sometimes and I wouldn't say a word or didn't know what to say. And I'd say, Lord, help me. Help me to come out of myself. Slowly Christ helped me come out of myself, to do what I'm doing today. God exists. God works in God's way.

I thought for a while that maybe God was calling me to the religious life. I heard about a men's order in the Anglican church called the Society of the Sacred Mission. They were running a parish down in South Tuggeranong, and so I moved down to Tuggeranong. My parents had moved to the coast because of my dad's health. I had to find somewhere to live, so I was renting by myself or with groups.

I went and checked out Saint Mary's in the Valley because things were sort of slowing down at Saint Alban's at the time. I knocked on the door at Saint Mary's and was involved with Saint Mary's for a long time in the singing group. I was still exploring what was God's will for me. God was tapping me on the shoulder about becoming become a priest. And I said, no. No way. I'm terrible at studies. How can I become a priest? Impossible. Well, God's got a way of things. I spent almost two years as a novice in Melbourne and then Adelaide with the Society for the Sacred Mission and in the end decided it wasn't for me.

I had to give up my job in the public service when I went in, taking twelve months leave without leave, eventually resigned and then came back to Canberra unemployed and back living with mum and dad, then looking after a house in Chifley for friends going overseas. I got a few jobs through Templine, one with Australian passports, processing Australian passport applications. Through that, I eventually got a job working for the British High Commission in the consular section doing passports and then visas. I did that for eight years. While I was down at Saint Mary's they started a bit of a preaching program under a program called the Neo Catechumenal Way, which was then in the Anglican church. Its origins were Catholic coming from Spain in the nineteen sixties through a man called Kiko Aguelo, now 86 and a woman called Carmen Hernandez. They heard the words of Saint Charles de Foucauld saying, go to the poor. You will find Christ amongst the poor. Kiko went to live in the shanty towns around Madrid in Spain.

The program starts with preaching done by a team they call catechists, who are teachers, older brothers and sisters in the faith in Christ. I was part of teams giving those catechists. These teachings of Christianity through the Way, as they often call themselves, are worldwide. I was involved with the Neo Catechumenate Way for over thirty years. I'm a priest because of them. They had, like all organisations, good and bad things, they can get a bit cultish, which is why I'm not with them today, which is a great pity.

Behind my brain was always, okay, Lord. I still sense this call to the priesthood. Which one? Anglican or Catholic? The Catholic one won, so sorry, Anglicans. The Catholic church had seminaries throughout the world to train men of all ages, who they see as called to the priesthood. We become diocesan missionary priests. I was sent to Perth after doing a stint of itinerancy as we call it, announcing the gospel. There was no monetary support, always reliant on the providence of God. I left the British High Commission in 1998 and spent six months in Darwin working for a parish at Humpty Doo.

I started my priestly studies in Perth after going to Italy to place near Portis and Georgia where we do what is called a Convivence, which is, living together and sorting out your call. You go there prepared to go to train for the priesthood to go anywhere in the world, and I mean anywhere in the world. I thought, oh, it'd be nice to go Europe. But no, God had different plans.

I ended up in Perth. I trained for the Catholic priesthood at Notre Dame University and Redemptoris Mater, mother of the Redeemer, which all the seminaries of the Neo Catechumenate Way are called after. I did five years, including a stint in Broome, waiting for the parish there in February 2002.

I wasn't sure about continuing so I came back to Canberra unemployed, got a job with the South African Embassy doing consular work, passports and visas. The Way have an annual meeting of all the communities around Australia. As the Way is now so big around Australia, they have two or three of these meetings initially and at one of these meetings I felt the call, God tapped me on the shoulder.

I was ordained a deacon and priest in February 2009.

I'm going back to the trans bit because it's interesting. I've been a feminist all my life. I've always been on the side of the girls. I always think differently to men. A few times in the seminary, some of the boys got a bit rambunctious, and I kept saying to myself, it's just too much testosterone around here. Even though I was mostly living with men, I actually craved the company of women, and there were a few women working in the office.

I worked in Kelmscott in Perth for four years as a deacon, assistant priest, and then parish priest. At that time there was a bit of antagonism in the Parish and I was asked to take it over. I said Lord, I don't know what I'm doing now. But God provided. God helped me. I made mistakes, and it was okay. We built a new house, a presbytery or manse as they call it in the Uniting Church, and a new church.

My father got very sick in 2016. I'd left the parish in Perth and I was in mission, not in a parish, and running a small team doing evangelisation in Adelaide, Western New South Wales including Broome. In 2011, when I was home my father had a major heart attack. They were living at Batemans Bay at the time. Thankfully, I was there. I had the car because I had driven across and was there for a few weeks. In 2016, he had surgery again. I came over for two weeks after Easter, but as he had complications I had to stay.

That's how I come back to Canberra. The Way and my Archbishop in Perth suggested offering my services to the Catholic diocese while here, so I did. I was assistant priest at Western Creek, Saint John Vianney, and Saint Jude's. Then I went to the Cathedral as an assistant priest and then running the Saint Christopher's Cathedral Parish for a year. I had a short stint out at Charnwood and then came down the other end of the valley again. I was in South

Tuggeranong as assistant priest in the Catholic parish there, and then finally, Dickson.

COVID hit in 2020. Now the thing is because of who I knew I was and because of the bullying, I developed what I used to call emotional shields, which have good and bad effects. One bad effect is you hide yourself. I hid myself for fifty years. But just little bit of me came out. During that time, I noticed my emotional shield stopped working, and this is a problem. In COVID we were isolated. I was working from home, which I was used to anyway. For Sunday mass we did a recording on a Friday with just a few of us, parish priest, me, one or two others. It was put up on YouTube for the parish. Each of us would take turns leading it or giving the homily.

I had this gender issue I've had all my life, which had bothered me. I started thinking and praying. The Way already knew about this issue, because I had told them previously and I kept talking to them. In early 2021, my community was at a stage that during Advent and Lent, we met for morning prayer, and as the priest I would be leading the morning prayer. We would have a time of silent meditation and I was thinking about me, praying to God about me. *What shall I do about this issue, about my gender? I need to do something.*

Through COVID, I did a lot of research through YouTube. I do a lot of research before I do things to find out the good and the bad things. I needed to talk to somebody about this. After Easter in 2021, I got in touch with Meridian and had some useful counselling. I only had four sessions with a lovely lady, and it revealed I had a lot of fears, called internal transphobia. I remember the session. She went through a whole lot of questions. One of them, she asked, and she first said, don't think about this, Andrew, which was my previous name. What gender are you? I said, female. I've always been female all my life. I knew this as a kid, being through the training for the priesthood, even trying to live as a guy.

Then I said, oh, bloody hell. I'm in the worst occupation if you realise you're a trans female, a Catholic priest and having to be male. What am I going to do about that? Well, Lord, what are we going do about that?

I spent eighteen months trying to pull myself together psychologically, trying to put the two together, putting the shields up. I mean, I'm very good at shields and appear to be this male, a Catholic priest. By this time, I was a hospital chaplain, which I loved. But then but I'm also trans and looking at it, do I want to transition?

How can I live with this? I talked to a doctor and actually started hormone replacement therapy, estrogen, still living as a man, as a priest. In September 2022, it came to a head as other people in the Way found out, and they weren't happy. They said you can't go that way, the words of that effect. And I said, "well, yes. I hear you, Well, I've got to be me."

I talked with a good couple in Monash. I am the godparent to one of their sons and was encouraged to go away and pray, think and make a decision, to go in one direction or the other. Is it the priesthood or is it you're transgender? I couldn't go away because dad was ill at the time. I said to myself I've got to be me. I'm a priest and I'm transfeminine. Now what are the ramifications? About this time, I started coming to TUC Rainbow Fellowship, initially black clericals and as a guy. This was one of my safe places where I could relax, be myself and didn't have to put barriers up. This is why I am still here.

The Way told my Bishops in Perth and I spoke with one Bishop and felt I was heard. He told me to write a letter explaining everything. I wrote a letter, ten pages, and sent it to the Archbishop. He rang me and we talked. He told me he was going to give me 12 months leave from public ministry and in that time I would be lay. You can live as a lay person in whatever gender you choose and then let's see. I was given some financial support.

In February 2023 I resigned and started living full time myself, not as a priest and looking for a job. God provided a job through a person at TUC. On hearing I was needing a job, she suggested

I send her my resume. I went for an interview. I tried a few other things that I call black holes during that time, like a hospitality course. Some months later a temporary job was offered from the interview, so I went back to the Public Service. My support from the Catholic Church and some savings got me through that waiting time. God provided. I like the job and its interesting.

I am on the road of gender transition, discovering myself. I have many good friends who pointed things out to me saying you need to change this. Andi you walk like a guy you need to walk like a woman. I needed help with clothes and thankfully there were the Red Dove ladies who helped me. I was not used to colour after having to wear black all the time as a priest. Now I am finding my style. It is not easy for trans people both in Australia and worldwide. Why are people transphobic? Is it ignorance, their education. I was very frightened at our last Election. Would my rights be taken away?

I have just returned from a trip as a woman to Turkey. We had a women's group of 12. The guide was great and three of the women knew and the others didn't and assumed I was female. I enjoyed the trip and I had good chats with one lady who was a nurse involved in a lot of ministry and working with people psychologically and that was helpful. I had surgery a year ago which means I don't have what I call the male bits anymore.

I really didn't know what I was going to say in my talk to you today. I had a brief plan and points and I think I have covered everything except preaching. Talking to a group of people is always a work of God. I have preached here on several occasions, and my catholic experience comes out at times.

I'm still trying to figure out what God is doing with my life here. I have all this training and wondering what am I going to do? Some people have said why not become an Anglican minister. God hasn't answered that one yet, but I have learned to wait. When God is ready, God will answer and point me in the direction. God provides and every day I stand with God and say God help me. Help me to be me. Help me to transition, help me to love. Help me to turn out some good news of this beautiful relationship all of us can have with Jesus in the power of the Holy Spirit. The love of God is for all of us.

Folllowing Andi's talk , the following prayer for Andi was offered.

God, we know that you call us to be followers of you, to be followers of Christ. We know that Andi is and always will be a priest. God, we pray that you continue to guide her and call her into ministry where you will have her serve. God, we thank you for her vulnerability, her strength and courage, and we ask that you continue to bless her in her life and ministry. Amen

4

LIFE'S QUESTIONS ALONG THE WAY

My name is Cathy and like many others, my faith journey started with my childhood. As the second in a family of four children, I was born and raised in Canberra. My parents followed the Christian traditions associated with Anglicanism (and in their own childhoods, of Methodism). Their commitment to their faith varied to some extent as it does with most of us! In keeping with a nominally 'Christian' country of those times, my parents certainly ensured our Christian upbringing as children. I remember early childhood prayers at bedtime, the telling of bible stories (such as the 'Lost Sheep' and the 'Prodigal Son'), and the saying of grace at dinner time. Also, as a young child I had the positive experience of the kindness and warmth of Sunday School teachers. I don't recall much about content or doctrine – but simply warmth and goodness. This speaks to me about how children's and young people's ministry can have a lasting impact when it truly reflects God's love. While I have felt close to God at times and at other times less close, my early Christian upbringing certainly fostered a sense of God's love and presence with me that I have had throughout my life.

However, like most of us, I have always asked questions on the purpose and meaning of life. I have endeavoured to probe the 'answers' Christianity has to offer. To some extent my mother also asked such questions which we sometimes discussed. Yet she was not one to study the bible as such, while I was intrigued by the bible and its interpretation. Nevertheless, my mother maintained some connection to the Church throughout her long life. Also, after retiring from a high-achieving career in the Public Service, my father in his sixties faced his own mortality. In doing so, I was very aware of how he sought reconnection with Christian friends from university – in particular, those associated with the fellowship that he had enjoyed as part of the Student Christian Movement (SCM) at university. It seems to me that we all want to make some sense of the mystery of where we have come from and where we are going. My father was certainly interested in seeking out Christian 'answers'. This promoted within me a greater determination to ask and explore questions of faith throughout my life.

As a young person, I became involved with the youth group at our church. In my university days, I became a member of both the Evangelical Union (EU) and the Student Christian Movement (SCM). I was impressed with the enthusiasm of the EU with its focus on the 'saving' work of Jesus and of evangelism. But I also appreciated the SCM's focus on social justice and in relating the Christian faith to contemporary issues. Both emphases have their place and can be related to how best to follow Christ in the modern world. In this regard, of central importance is the question: 'Who is Jesus Christ for me today?' Back in Jesus' time, and as recorded in the Gospels, it resonates with the challenging question that Jesus asks his disciples: "Who do people say that I am?" And they answered him, "John the Baptist; and others, Elijah; and still others, one of the prophets." He asked them, "But who do you say that I am?" Peter answered him, "You are the Messiah." [i.e., the 'Christ'] (Mark 8: 27b – 29).

After my university years I met my husband, John, who also had a church background. He was sympathetic to Christianity but not a regular churchgoer. However, John was a caring and gentle person who often emulated the 'upside-down' values of the Kingdom (or God's reign) – and often in more ways than myself! During these years, I drifted away from church attendance, although I quite often found myself defending Christianity from the criticism of others! But I think the big 'birth' and 'death' events (especially that of loved ones), can profoundly affect and change our perspectives. During my thirties, the experience of giving birth to three precious sons greatly enhanced my sense of the God-given wonderment of new life. I renewed and nurtured my faith as part of a local Anglican community – becoming a leader in different activities and ministries. Like many young parents, I attempted to balance my life in caring for our children and enjoying part-time work which was centred on adult learning at the Canberra Institute of Technology.

There were many blessings in my thirties, but the sudden death of John from cancer in 1993 was a tremendous shock, sadness and upheaval for myself and our family. Similar to facing other hardships in our broken world, John's unexpected death was a challenge to my faith. Nevertheless, the prayer and on-going practical support from family, friends and the Christian community was inspiring. At times, I could 'accidently' encounter God's 'angels', that is, those people who seemed especially sent to me to meet my needs. Over the years, what has become obvious to me is that God's grace is practically expressed to us. That is, it is expressed through the 'hands' of those in touch with the life of God which is love and compassion (see 1 John 4:16).

Once I retired in my sixties, I had the opportunity to more fully explore all my questions by studying at St Marks for six years to gain my Master of Arts (Theological Studies). I studied many topics including: Christian doctrines; early Church history; the Old Testament; the New Testament; and practical or pastoral ministries. I gained many insights, but also realised that there are diverse perspectives and theologies in the scriptures, diverse expressions of Christianity, and many scholarly contested ideas! Theology invites continuing reflection on both the revelation and mystery of God. In examining the scriptures, one concept that I found helpful is that of the Quadrilateral Model. This model highlights how our faith is informed around four main sources: tradition, scripture, reason and experience. Interestingly, the difference between Christian faith traditions can be understood in the emphasis given to one or more of these aspects. The model is also useful in interpreting biblical passages – especially those focused on contentious issues! It leads us into considering a biblical passage in the light of our tradition, reason and experience. Also, a thoughtful strategy is to examine scripture using a 'lens' of God's love. (And more specifically, the love of God as revealed in Christ's teaching, actions and 'saving' work of reconciliation).

I think God appreciates a questioning faith that seeks understanding. God wants us to use our minds (albeit, our hearts as well!), and the discernment of the Spirit to critically engage with scripture. We all select and highlight certain texts of scripture that are meaningful to us. A favourite of mine expresses that we are "To do justice, and to love kindness and to walk humbly with your God" (Micah 6:8).

After completing my theological studies, my new learning and reflections led me to feel dissatisfied with my local evangelical Anglican Church – my church community of almost forty years! This was exacerbated by a change in leadership of our church which encompassed the conservative views of the Sydney diocese, including denying women full leadership roles. Although I still retain many close ties with people and friends from this church, I decided to take the plunge and look elsewhere. I wanted to be part of a church that among other qualities valued scholarly thinking, engagement with contemporary issues, social-justice, and inclusiveness. The website of Tuggeranong Uniting Church (TUC) communicated this ethos and in a vibrant way! I have not been disappointed from joining TUC (and the Uniting Church). From the moment I stepped through the doors, I was warmly welcomed! Over time, I hope to make a greater contribution to the life of TUC.

Whilst many of us may be able to celebrate a particular 'conversion' event, I nevertheless think it is our on-going relationship with Christ – with God, which is central to a life of faith. And pivotal to this, is not only scripture, but a life of prayer and of action. In prayer we can intimately communicate with God, and receive God's grace, wisdom and direction. But as we sometimes think, this 'direction' can seem problematic. It is easy to feel overwhelmed by the world's significant problems, including war, poverty and gross inequality, injustices, and the disastrous effects of climate change and environmental degradation. Yet God's presence is with us wherever we are. And where God is there is hope. Jesus has proclaimed the liberating 'good news' of the Kingdom (see Luke 4:16-21). And God invites us to participate in his transforming work of renewal, healing and wholeness – of creating a Christ-shaped world.

Perhaps because I am a gardener, I like to consider the image of the sunflower. To me, the sunflower reminds us of the importance of hope, and also, how our love for God needs to be constantly renewed. The bright yellow flower conveys joy and looks to the light. It resists the darkness. It constantly turns to God's light, love, justice-orientation, generosity and hope. Like the sunflower, we need to "constantly turn our lives towards God as a sunflower constantly turns its face to the sun". (Pritchard, J. in Shepherd, Greene & Treweek, 2019, p. 33). And like the sunflower we need to radiate the brightness of God's love.

5

LIONS, SCORPIONS AND FIG TREES

Blessed is she who has believed that the Lord would fulfill his promises to her! Luke 1:45

My name is Eileen and I thought I was going to find the right fella, get married and have kids before I was 23, and then I thought, before I was 25... okay fine, before I'm 30 then. And then 30 came and went. And I was doing the math and the timelines. I went on dates, but there wasn't anybody that I was really interested in actually dating. There hasn't been since I told God that I was sick of 'friendships' and dates that never went anywhere. I said to God that I didn't want a boyfriend unless it would be with the man I marry. Mmm... yeah, don't say stuff like that unless you're really prepared for what it may mean. So I haven't been interested in anyone since that little chat with God. And whilst for the most part I've been okay with that (albeit lonely at times), I wasn't okay with the thought of being childless.

Late one night I was especially feeling the longing. I prayed "Lord, If having children isn't part of your plan for me, then take it away. I don't want this want if it's not going to happen." And I was pretty blunt with God... "because it's kind of mean to give someone this desire and then not fulfil it." The next morning I awoke from a dream, the kind that you think must have a meaning to it. In the dream I was in a new house and unpacking a box of mis-matched crockery, when I thought I'll just go check on my daughter. I could see a dark haired girl soundly asleep, but at the end of the bed was a scorpion. The dream ended there but I woke up with no fear. I thought about that dream all day, what did it mean? That night I opened up my bible, and there was the verse 'If a child asks for an egg do you give him a scorpion? Of course not'. Luke 11:12

(summarised).

From then, I knew I had to just trust God, that this was a promise of my future. I also knew I had to do what I could do to prepare myself for this future. Mentally, spiritually and physically.

I was struggling with some pelvic pain around this time. I have Polycystic Ovarian Syndrome (PCOS) which is an endocrine disorder, and this particular pain could have been related to that or to something else. I'd just had one minor procedure to check things and thin my thickened uterus lining (to help prevent endometrial cancer). I was still having awful pains and was due for another procedure the following week. After an awful night from these pains, I had a dream. In the dream I was in a large hilly field where a lion was stalking me, I felt afraid as I couldn't get to the safe space. The safe space was in a valley where my friends and family were waiting and were worried for me. I wasn't sure how to get there with this lion following me each way I turned. Then a tiger came right up next to me and I just knew this tiger was safe. So by the side of the tiger, he led me to the safe space.

I had that dream on my mind all day. That night I went to my bible-study group and without me having said anything of my dream or of my medical situation, one of the guys said he had this verse on his mind all day (after reading it that morning), and he read this verse "Give all your worries and cares to God, for he cares about you. Stay alert! Watch out for your great enemy, the devil. He prowls around like a roaring lion, looking for someone to devour. Stand firm against him, and be strong in your faith... So after you have suffered a little while, he will restore, support, and strengthen you, and he will place you on a firm foundation. All power to him forever! Amen. 1 Peter 5:7-11 (summarised)

I then told the group the dream I'd had and the pain I was experiencing and of the upcoming medical procedure. I'd mentioned to the group that I don't know how a tiger came into it. That Sunday one of the members said she had been pondering 'why a tiger' too, and then it came to her. Tigers have stripes, and so did Jesus. 'By his stripes you are healed.'

I had this second ordinary, minimal risk procedure on the Friday. Then I woke up in the ICU. My heartrate had gone extremely low and I required some CPR. Thank God I had that tiger leading me safely away from the lion. I was healed of the excruciating pelvic pain also.

A year or so later I was looking to buy a house and I knew I wanted a house that was future proof. It wasn't a house for me just in this period of my life, but a house that would house my future family (with no scorpions!).

I found a house that ticked my 'must have' boxes, and whilst I really liked this house, I was still unsure if I was doing the right thing. At a crucial time of offers and re-offers I went for a long walk. I prayed and said to God, "this is it. Is this the right house for me, do I actually buy this house, am I doing the right thing?". That night I was reading my 'Bible in a Year' (which I'm always on the wrong day), and there was a verse with fig tree (probably Proverbs 27:18). I then read my Daily Devotional and there was a second verse about a fig tree. Though the fig tree does not bud, and no fruit on the vines... yet I will exult in the Lord; I will rejoice in the God of my salvation!... (summarised) Habakkuk 3:17-19. There's not many verses about fig trees, and to have two in one evening was thought provoking to me. Because here's the thing; this house that I was prayerfully considering to buy had two fig trees. And as I would later find out, one of those fig trees does not fruit.

In my new lovely new home, I felt God was telling me to 'Wait'. The future family you want isn't here just yet and just because it hasn't happened yet, doesn't mean it won't. But waiting for my future family, didn't mean I had to sit on my hands and do nothing. I could prepare myself for the life that I dreamed of.

My pastor once said 'Put your hope into faith and put your faith into action'. The Reverend Al Green in his big Memphis soul voice said "you can pray until you faint! But if you don't get up and do something, God ain't gonna put it in your mouth." So, what am I going to get up and do? What action am I going to take?

I looked into overseas adoption (virtually impossible for a solo person and very expensive). I looked into local foster-care (our city does not typically do adoption). In 2019 I signed up to be a foster carer and did the very thorough checks and training. I cared for children in 'Out of Home Care' in a crisis and respite capacity. Some children I took into my home for a few nights and others for six months. I got to watch one pre-teen girl grow and mature over several years of semi-regular weekends and the odd week here and there. I cared for children from 4 days old to nearly 14 years old. All these children come with some trauma in one form or another. There were some pretty challenging times, and some broken windows, but also fun and rewarding times. However, being single and working full-time meant that potential forever care (e.g. 18year care orders) of young children was not really feasible. I wouldn't be eligible for any sort of leave other than my work recreational leave or long service leave. If I used that leave and then the child was re-unified with their biological family (which is ultimately the goal), then I would not have that leave again to use again in the near future.

I still haven't met the right fella, and I'm not getting any younger. I was feeling the tick tock of that biological clock. Now I can say looking back that I was given the gift of desperation. But back then it just felt like despair. I was still doing the math and the timelines.

You know when you get multiple non connected people saying similar things in a short period of time, you think maybe I should think about what they're saying. I was also having some recurring dreams about corridors and doors. I was also feeling like God wasn't saying 'wait' anymore.

I believe that God doesn't want you to just sit around, he's not going to bring the doors themselves to you. You have to actually walk up to the door and turn the handle or at least knock. So I did.

I went to my former gynaecologist, now fertility specialist and had a few tests. With my history, age (then 39) and just 3 very small eggs, she gave me about a 5% chance (with IVF). She said here in Canberra it's a 9-12 month wait for donors. She said "Eileen, don't wait that long, get up to Sydney where they don't have a wait and do it very soon". Try a few rounds of IUI (interuterine insemination) in Sydney to start with and then go back to her in Canberra for IVF.

During this time I felt like I had to just keep walking through those doors. I asked God to close any doors on my path if this wasn't his plan and purpose. He didn't. There were many times that those doors could have stayed locked up tight. Remember I was given 5% chance by my fertility specialist. I had PCOS, I was 39, and IUI's in general have 10-20% success rate each round. The chance of miscarriage is also higher in those with PCOS.

I walked up to the figurative door, turned the handle and walked through the door. Miraculously I became pregnant first IUI and carried to term. At 40years old I was blessed with a beautiful dark haired daughter. I am so, so blessed.

When I asked God to take away the desire for children if it wasn't his plan for me, he gave me that dream with a daughter and a scorpion. He then gave me the verse. "If a child asks for an egg, do you give him a scorpion? Of course not!" I asked him for a child and he gave me my daughter.

God gave me literal dreams and he would back them up with an associated verse so that I would know that this was his promises to me. He revealed his promises to me and fulfilled them.

P.S. I'm still praying for the right fella to join our little family.

Believe that he has a good plan and purpose for your life. Take steps to go after it. The bible says knock and the door will be opened. Go up to that door and if it opens, you still need to walk through it. Turn your hope into faith and your faith into action.

I waited patiently for the lord, and he turned to me and heard my cry.
Psalm 40.1

6

MY WALK WITH GOD

Isaiah 40:31 *But they that wait upon the Lord shall renew their strength, they shall mount up with wings as eagles they shall run and not be weary, and they shall walk and not faint.*

My name is Elizabeth and my personal walk with God really didn't start until I was nineteen. As young adult I attended a service at the Lyceum theatre, the speaker Dr Robert Schuller an American Evangelist, brought the word of God alive to me. After hearing what he said, something clicked that night and I realised that God was real, he did love me, that's what I was missing and that he would accept me just as I was, with all my weakness, troubles, abilities, and that he would forgive me for everything. I could be part of His family. I had a purpose in life for being here and I accepted Him into my life as my Father, friend, and saviour, trusting that he would always be with me.

Let me fill you in with a bit about my life's journey. Going back to my childhood, I was quite shy and very insecure and not a lot of confidence as a kid growing up. I always tried to ensure things were done and right, so we wouldn't get into trouble, although I did test my parents quite a bit.

I grew up in Lithgow, with two sisters and two brothers. I played a lot of sport, managed to get through school, got a job in the local department store as a secretary (wasn't very good at it) and then changed to the accounts department and this is where I fitted in.

Growing up I didn't have a faith, as I know it today, even though mum took us to church. Dad was against the church and everything it stood for, sometimes it was hard as there was conflict and controversy about church and other things in our home. You never knew what would happen in our home from day to day. I did learn about God and Jesus, through memory verses and bible stories while I was at Sunday School, but never related it to my life, or understood it. It was just something we did each Sunday.

Church was strict back then, you had to be good all the time, (you got told on the way to church to be good or else) very hard for us kids to be able to do. As a teenager I went to youth group and found this a safe place, a refuge you might say, where I was accepted, a good outlet for me from home, but still didn't comprehend the God stuff. One thing that has always stuck with me. I remember one Sunday morning walking down the right-hand aisle of the church with my eyes to the ground so I wouldn't be noticed and then a gentleman from the church, stopped me and spoke softly to me and said, "always look up and see where you are going, God is walking with you." I never really understood it then, but after many years, and reflecting on life I can see now what this gentleman said to me back then, has been with me all these years. God has always been there walking with me.

Meeting Tony was a significant step forward in life, as he was a Christian, he went to church, but this then started a tug of war within me. We did attend church together, and he tried to get me to understand, who God was, and that He loved me. How could God be in my life, and love me, but let me grow up with such struggles in life.

Tony's family was very different to mine, they accepted me. They showed me a different way of family life, how life could be filled with love, compassion, a mum and dad who did care and were interested in what you did, everyone getting on together most of the time, doing family things together, chats around the meal table, family picnic, playing card games. God was a major part of the family life; His dad was a lay preacher.

As time passed by Tony was transferred to Sydney from Lithgow. I was alone once more, struggling with life and work, trying to understand what was happening. I was not coping, garbling with life, really didn't want to live any more, not knowing what to do or where to go and after a time realising, I did want to survive and move on. What next, move to Sydney or stay where I am? This was a huge decision to make, needing to get a job, a place to live. I moved to Sydney. Wow... I had never moved before, very scared of what would happen, a country girl moving to the city without knowing anyone there, except Tony, and having to find a job to be able to survive. How will I cope? This was all very hard. Tony kept telling me to Trust God and that he would guide me through life, but I couldn't understand what he was talking about, as so much was happening that I had no control over.

Little did I know that God had things in hand, despite my doubts and fears. I got a job in the accounts department at Central Methodist Mission from my first interview. The mission was going through the process moving to union which I was involved with. I experienced seeing how God worked in the lives of the people that I worked with. God opened my eyes. It was during that time that we attended the Robert Schuller Event, and this is where my walk with God really started.

After marriage we moved to different places with Tony's work, to Narromine, Bourke, and Bega before coming to Canberra, where I didn't want to shift to. The weather was always cold, it had snowed the month before we came, in October mind you. We thought we'd only be here a few years, 30 something years later, we are on the move once again.

Through these great years, we were blessed with 3 beautiful children, as family life evolved, there has been lots of joy, laughter, tears, celebrations, family holidays, and blessing, seeing the milestones and our children grow and become matured adults, rising above all that they have been faced with. Our family has grown with weddings, extended families, and 6 wonderful grandchildren, and I have had the opportunity to share life with all of them. I loved staying at home with the children as they grew up, being the homemaker, helping the kids with homework, a taxi driver taking the kids to soccer, calisthenic, gymnastics and Girls Brigade. I did go back to work when the children got older. I tried to be best mum that I could be, not always being successful, (I think the kids could testify to this). I did have lots of guidance and help along the way, especially from Tony's mum. We raised our children within God's community, I had to trust in Him and eventually let them make their own decision about their own faith and accept it.

Our family attended the Uniting Church in the different towns, being involved within a caring community was wonderful, where we were very welcomed, as they accepted us transit people, as often the town folk didn't as we weren't born there. During these years schoolteachers, bankies, police and minister's families supported each other, though many milestones of life, sharing many meals and celebrations, often relying on each other during difficult times. Friendships grew strong, as none of us had extended families. We still have many of these friendships today, even though you may not see them very often, we are able to pick up where we left off.

Learning to live in different towns and environments was also a challenge but rewarding as well, understanding the different cultures, and getting involved in the different communities' activities. I joined playgroups with other mums and kids, found this a great support. I went to TAFE to study a sewing course focusing on children's clothes.

Tony loved gardening, as we worked together, we landscaped the gardens in the different homes we have lived in. Going to bible studies played a significant part of life, as I learnt more about God, and understanding how God could love me so much, that he gave his life for me. Even though I couldn't quite comprehend why someone would do this for me.

Finding time to spend with God daily wasn't easy, I wasn't disciplined in this, as many of you know, raising children, look after the home, your hands where always busy with something, or your mind was going round and around thinking, and other obstacles getting in the way, I fought with this for many years, I would often stray, detouring from God, not feeling close to Him, like sheep wandering off the path, eventually coming back. I had to learn the significance of making time, having that quiet time with him, pondering his world, unpacking his word, just spend time with Him, and this would get me through the days, or whatever was happening. I now know that if you don't spend time with God, life takes a dive and Satan manoeuvres his way in and distracts you.

In my darkest days, when postnatal depression set in and life was a challenge to cope with, some days you just didn't. The challenges of raising a family, not having extended family around, moving from town to town, having to settle in and start a fresh again, this was huge for me each time we moved, as I am not good with change.

But God was always there, I had to make time with Him, listen for his voice, walk, and talk with him, read his word, and accept things. I had to learn to stop trying to be in control, and hand things to God to deal with, but I would then often take it back, hand it back again and this often happened over and over. Learning to leave everything in His hands. A very hard lesson to learn.

Life took many turns, lots of experiences, ups and downs, you think life is going along smoothly and then something happens, childhood challenges, kid getting hurt, visits to hospital, challenges with extended family, no money to pay the bills, car breaks down, just everyday life occurring. But He has always seen us through, often not the way I thought.

Prayer was something that I struggled with for many years, always thought my prayers were never good enough didn't have the right words, happy to pray in silence, not out loud, thought people would judge me on what I said. He had to work on me over many years, I had to accept and realise what I said in pray was good enough for God and he didn't worry how or what I said he just knew what was in my heart. Even today I sometime still stumble a little with this.

My faith has been rocked several times over the years, including Tony's fight with pneumonia and pleurisy in our early years of marriage, and the passing of his dad. One of the major crises within our family was when Leanne, our eldest daughter, got sick with cancer, Non-Hodgkin Lymphoma at the age of 15. Even though she had been sick on and off for about two years, doctors didn't diagnose her until then. We didn't really know anything about cancer. What a turmoil in her life and ours, going through treatments, doctors' appointments, coping with side effects from the treatment, and Leanne being a teenager growing up. Life wasn't fair, but she was amazing through the ordeal, wanting to keep life as normal as possible. Tony's family was great, being there helping when they could, on the other end of the phone, (no mobiles back then.)

I was the one who didn't cope very well. I kept asking God why, how could he allow our daughter to go through these agonizing things. As a parent you want to fix it, make it better, but I just couldn't, I was helpless in this situation, I had to lean heavily on God and others, we had many, talks, prayed, cried, nights seemed to be worst times. Finally realising that God had her in the palm of His hand, I had to give her over to Him and leave it, trust him, this was very, very hard to accept, I just had too. And he did, with the support of all the doctors and nurses, she recovered and went on to have a normal young adult life.

But then life took many turns for her, and she battled breast cancer for many years, lots more treatments, go into remission, but it would come back again, three more times, each getting worse until her body gave out. She fought so hard to overcome all the battles that she faced and still wanted to keep living as normal a life as possible. We had many in depth conversations about God, faith, Heaven, and hell, coming to terms with what was happening, especially as it got closer to her facing death. She was struggling with her own faith. All I could do was listen and remind her that God loved her, had a place for her in his kingdom, she only had keep believing in Him, this was a testing time for me as well.

I could never make it OK for her I just had to be there, do what mums do, keep her in prayer, listen, be on the end of the phone or at her bedside. I kept questioning God, I never felt he answered me with a straight answer. When my faith was lacking, fear set in, often feeling helpless I had to trust, know he was in control. The bible verse "Be Still and know that I am God became real to me", as I had to be still, trust him, accept his comfort.

Even though we knew what the outcome was going to be, her passing was still devesting /heart wrenching and hard on all of us. I understood this more during that first week, when one night, feeling very sad and lonely, I reached out to God, felt his overwhelming presence enfolding me in his arms, held and comforted me, as He spoke these words, I am here with you, I felt at peace then.

We were very much blessed and supported by this church's caring community, with prayers, encouragement, hugs, people offering help, meals. Throughout these times we were very grateful to everyone.

There are days when I feel overwhelmed with too much to do, not enough time, trying to fit too much into my day or week, and doing things on my own. Being task oriented, I like being organised and I don't deal with conflict very well, just want to resolve the problem as I don't like seeing people get hurt. At times this has impacted my home/ work/life balance. This has often got me into deep waters, focusing on the task at hand and leaving other thing behind.

As my faith and confidence has grown over many years God has been working within me to transform me, he still has a way to go, from being the person I was, to the person he wants me to be. I have had to learn many lessons, stop, sit back, do a lot of praying, share the load, appreciating what others can offer, and seeing how they have enriched my life.

I have been given the roles of leadership in different areas within my workplace even though sometimes it has been stressful. It has strengthened and challenged me working in a very worldly environment. Begin able to be open and honest about my faith has brought conflict and provided me opportunities to stand up for my Christian values and not caving into what has been asked of me.

We have been part of TUC's church community for many years and it has enriched my life. Being supported and part of a wider family, sharing good time and bad, the opportunities of meals together and being part of women's bible studies, also being involved in my small group, for we have been together for a long time. Hearing His word spoken here, has enabled me to embrace the Holy Spirit and let God work within me.

Girls' Brigade has been a very significant part of my faith journey for many years, and the passion for it has grown over time. I became involved in GB when Leanne started and we lived in Melba, then we moved to south side of Canberra. Leanne and Melissa joined TUC Girls' Brigade, I started to help out and loved just coming along.

My involvement really started when they asked me to become a leader, I didn't think I could do that, me, be a leader, I didn't have the confidence so no way, but after lots of searching, encouragement and prayer, the voice in the back of my head, kept telling me, you can do this, step forward, and out of your comfort zone. I fought it for a while, I never thought I could step up to leadership as I was just an ordinary person with no amazing skills or attributes that shone out, I remember thinking how I could lead these girls, but God had other ideas.

I have learnt so much through Girls Brigade, he has given me the strength when I was lacking confidence, abilities to face challenges, encouraged me to be creative, gave me love to share with others, wisdom to plan, knowledge to impart, courage to step out of my comfort zone and peace to know that he can use ordinary people like me, to serve him in this ministry to achieve his mission wherever we are planted. He has put me in situations where I have had to rely on him fully as I couldn't have done it on my own. But He is the master potter, I am the clay as he is moulding me into the vessel that he wanted me to be.

We have had many amazing nights, some very loud and raucous, and some calm and quiet, others didn't work out so well, but we would still get through. I would often review our nights and think, how I could have done it better. I had been tired, had I put enough time into planning. He was always present watching over us. In taking everything to God in prayer I have received a bountiful number of answered prayer and blessings.

The verse from Isaiah has helped me a lot. Isaiah 40:31 But they that wait upon the Lord shall renew their strength, they shall mount up with wings as eagles they shall run and not be weary, and they shall walk and not faint.

I just love how Girls Brigade provides a safe and loving environment for all girls, really encourages them, allows them to be themselves, teaches new skills, accepts the girl's uniqueness, abilities, able to make new friends, also challenges them to step out of their comfort zone as well. I really enjoy sharing time with the girls, getting know them, having a chat, finding out how there week has been, learning new things, playing games and being creative.

It is a blessing to see girls achieve so much, when they mastered a new skill, and seeing what they can achieve. I love to see their faces when that Light bulb moment happens, and their confidence grows. See them receiving their awards at presentation night/ or Receiving Queens' Award for Pioneer Pin, and our supper sharing times.

I love to see the smiles on their faces enjoying the fun and laughter, and the many mums, dads/daughter nights we have had. Seeing our leaders stepping forward and out of their comfort zone and their dedication to the girls. Being part of a worldwide family is just amazing, people with a passion helping girls embrace life, and having Christian women for the girls to look up to and be inspired.

I am sure God had a path planned out for me and put me here, I am grateful that I have been able give back something back to Girls Brigade. It has given me so much, the opportunity to share in the lives of different leaders and many girls, here and across Australia and in the different GB roles I have had.

As we celebrated 35years of Girls Brigade a ministry of TUC, it has enabled hundreds of girls to learn about God and the love he has for each of them. Through the years many girls have come, some for a short period, some have stayed for a longer time, as girls' lives have been transformed and who are now enriching God's world.

We give thanks and praise to God for them all, past, present and for the Leadership, throughout our history. Together we have had lots of fun, laughter, craziness, sleepover, camps, tried new thing, made friends, shared in devotions, and created lasting memories, with our Girls Brigade families and friends. We give thanks to the TUC community for their support encouragement to all the girls and leaders. You just never know how much Girls Brigade impacts or touches the lives of girls, and the community.

Over the past 12months I have walked my own journey with breast cancer, it was hard to hear those words again in our family, breast cancer, as it had already taken our daughter, but finding out we got it early and a good prognosis, with all the new knowledge and treatment that is available and it could be cured.

Even with that knowledge, I still questioned God, why me? Stopping and spending time in his presence, I heard Him say you are now walking in her shoes, understanding more of what she went through, the treatment. I tried to keep positive, did have some dark days, even during them I always felt I would recover and be healed, that I would come out stronger than before, enabling me to continue with my life's journey.

I have had the opportunity to be involved with Christ centred inspiring women that God has put in my path along my journey, whom I have learnt, laughed, walked, and cried with, women from both the wider church community and my Girls Brigade family.

Where to from here, as we move north to the warmer climate, I am not sure what is install for me, or what lays ahead. A new home, new town, challenges to face, leaving family and church family, starting over once more. I know this will be heart reaching even though we know it is the right thing to, as many things have all fallen into place, this is God's doing and prayers have been answered.

God has been the light of my world; he has walked with me picked me up and carried me on many occasions when I haven't been able to see the light for the darkness. Jesus' light has aways shone through, it is when I put my trust in him that he brings the light to the day and all things come together.

I know my future is filled with hope, never being alone, as his Holy spirit dwells within, to have that confidence and boldness to step forward. I serve a faithful God, and he gives me His peace as we walk forward together.

And the I can rejoice in Him with all the blessing.

Cry with all the heartache

Have peace within myself.

Feel the relief from the tension when God is in control.

Praise the Father, Son and Holy Spirt for all that has been and is to come in my life.

7

AN UNUSUAL MINISTRY JOURNEY

I made promises at my son's baptism and they haunted me.

My name is Elizabeth and I grew up in the Lake Macquarie area near Newcastle, and this was where my faith journey began. I wasn't in a Christian household as such, but my mother had taught me prayers and hymns at a very young age. For example, I could sing "O Come All Ye Faithful" in the four languages she had learnt at school. I went to Sunday school and had scripture classes at school. I remember little of the scripture at school but do from Sunday school at the local presbyterian church that I attended most of my childhood. That was probably where my Christian faith started its formation.

I married early and didn't have much of an early working life. I had drifted away from the church as a teenager, but what brought me back was my eldest son's baptism. I had taken him back to the church I was married in, the same church my parents were married in. I was one of those people who followed this ridiculous tradition of going to a church where some family event has occurred. I had my son baptised there and made promises to bring him up in the Christian faith. Making these promises haunted me as I wasn't attending a church. At that point I decided to go back to St David's in Charlestown, the church of my childhood, a couple of suburbs away from where I lived and that worked for me.

I became more involved in St David's, teaching Sunday school and becoming a full member there. I took my children to the Sunday school and became quite close friends with a woman I worked with. I didn't get seriously involved with the Uniting Church until I became the Director of the Newcastle Youth Service, an outreach service of Hamilton Wesley Uniting Church in Newcastle. My involvement there influenced me a lot, particularly meeting street children and kids who were in a lot of trouble. I had previously worked in Drug and Alcohol as an educator and was quite creative in coming up with all sorts of programs and activities. My imagination has always been overactive and this helped me produce creative ideas that initiated new projects.

The next step for me was wanting to be involved in the Uniting Church more, having a pastoral role to the street kids, by being able to do baptisms and maybe marrying these kids. Tragically, sometimes we lost one to suicide. I wanted to be part of honouring their life and lead funeral services. These things led me to applying to be a candidate for ordained ministry, which was quite an unusual path at the time. The Newcastle Youth Service experience had a very strong impact on me and how I saw ministry. During this time, we acquired a property at Wollombi, a rural area forty minutes south of Cessnock, where we had sheep, a milking cow and chickens. This began my interest in sustainability which has carried through to the present time.

At that time, Uniting Theological College, required a prior degree, preferably in Arts. I had done this, though it had taken me 9 years to get my BA in Classics and Psychology. My first marriage had also broken up before entering college. Here I met John and married him after my graduation. After the college, I wanted to study more so enrolled in a Master's degree in Ancient History at Macquarie University. Having three children and working meant most of my Master's coursework was done at night (2 subjects a semester) and I probably wouldn't do that again, as it almost killed me. John and I settled into life in Sydney, attending Epping Uniting church, where my sustainability interests led to Plot to Pot dinners and my creative imagination to Biblical Cultural Days and a number of Christmas in July events as part of their Arts in Action program.

I had an unusual pathway with my ministry career, and it didn't look like that of most ordained ministers. When I had started college, my eldest son remained in Newcastle with his grandmother, finishing the last two years of Primary School, while the younger two came with me to Sydney. When I finally finished college, it was thought I was rather feral, too unconventional and outspoken; but my Presbytery eventually agreed to ordain me. I probably wore out the knees of my more conservative fellow students, who persisted in praying for me to become more conventionally Christian.

I was told there was no placement for me, no congregation, even though I had worked for 9 months as a student chaplain at Newington, a Uniting Church Boys School. They refused to consider me there for a vacancy because I was female. As the student minister/chaplain there I gained a lot of experience teaching classes, taking chapel services and other things. I found my own placement, as the school experience enabled me to apply for an advertised position at Ku-ring-ai High School as a chaplain. I got the position and the Presbytery at that time recognised it as a placement, and I was ordained. The three years there was tough going but I learnt a lot. I made many friends among the staff and ended up getting on really well with the students, probably because of my background in drug and alcohol and youth work. It was during this time I completed my master's degree and was then accepted for a PhD at Durham University.

John and I moved overseas for a year to Durham in the north of England, taking my three children with us. I was supervised by Professor Jimmy Dunn, a prominent New Testament scholar and it was a really great year. I met fellow research students and good faculty members and became immersed in researching the Gospel of Matthew. It also gave me to opportunity to do a lot of family history work which was a great interest to me as the Raine family came from Country Durham. On returning to Australia, there was still no placement for me, so I did supply ministry for Riverstone Uniting Church for 6 months. They wanted me to stay but it was not the right fit for me. They were quite a conservative congregation and we had grown together as long as we didn't talk politics or certain aspects of religion.

Instead, I applied for a job at Western Sydney Tenants Service

(WESTS.) It was a ministry of the then Board of Social Responsibility that later became Uniting. Reverend Harry Herbert was quite enamoured with the idea I was working there, because he would say I was the only one who could keep him in line when I was a table leader at Synod and would be fearless tackling out of line landlords! The work I did was like paralegal work, basically helping tenants who had got into trouble through owing rent, or who had not got their bonds back and or had landlords who refused to do repairs. I was the designated worker on a phone line twice a week as people rang in for advice. I also represented tenants at the Residential Tenancy Tribunal and spent a fair bit of time doing this.

I worked at WESTS for 3 years before I became really sick with an undiagnosed autoimmune disease. Eventually we learnt I have lupus and Sjogren's disease, which made me quite ill. I was unwell on returning from England and had to stop work on my doctoral research. It took two years to get diagnosed, during which time I was in and out of hospital. Autoimmune diseases tend to take a while to be diagnosed, as they initially present with many nebulous symptoms.

When I started to stabilise health-wise, I was attending Epping Uniting Church and they needed someone in the church office so I volunteered as part of my rehabilitation back to work. It was three hours, two days a week and I did the admin work required. However, because I was a Minister, I soon began writing liturgies and other things at the request of the minister there and so that eased me back into church work. I ended up becoming the supply minister there when their minister became unwell and had to leave. This became my first Intentional Interim Ministry, where I was instrumental in combining the Oxford and Chester Street congregations. I had taken the IIM course, but really, I knew very little about how to go about combining two churches. But I gave it a go, often flying by the seat of my pants.

Working at Epping was a big job following my ill health. I remember the first meeting we had there. We had u-shaped sets of pews with Oxford Street on one side and Chester Street on the other side. It was a very difficult meeting. Some people were shouting and shaking their fists at one another. The two churches were a hundred yards apart and that is why the presbytery thought they should be together, and I think rightly so. One had been a Congregational church and the other Methodist church and despite that many people knew each other and were good friends, they thought of themselves as very different. It was hard going but eventually we got there and they are now happily together at the Chester Street site as Epping Uniting Church.

Following Epping, John and I went to Wauchope for five years in a shared ministry placement. We shared 50% as Presbytery Ministers and 50% as the Wauhope Congregation Minister position, but due to various ministry departures our time there later saw us also doing some supply ministry in the area to take us to full time. At Wauchope, we established an Aboriginal youth group, which we enjoyed greatly and learnt so much about aboriginal culture as we got to know them and their families.

Towards the end of our time at Wauchope, I came to Canberra to do another Intentional Interim Ministry, as I was asked by the Canberra Region Presbytery ministers to consider working with Canberra City church. My eldest son was living in Canberra, and I had just had a grandchild born so I saw this as a good chance to get to know my grandson. John then took a job in Western Australia and on finishing the Canberra job I joined him in Perth and took on yet another interim ministry position at Star Street Uniting in one of the suburbs in Perth. There were some factions in the congregation but during my time there the church grew a lot and we did various different and creative things.

My daughter and granddaughter were in Perth and I was able to see them a lot more. However, when my father had a heart attack, I realised I was a long way from family, and if he was going to die, I probably wouldn't get there in time to say goodbye. I was also missing the east coast and my family so when the Canberra Region Presbytery told me as part of the plan to lure me back that Tuggeranong Uniting was a possibility, I jumped at the chance. I flew to Canberra to talk to Tuggeranong and go to my grandson's third birthday.

I spent most of that Saturday talking with the Tuggeranong Joint Nominating Committee and the rest is history. I have spent 5 years at Tuggeranong Uniting and it is the best placement I could have asked for. When I started, I always knew that it would be my final placement though I wasn't sure how many years I had left in me with my ongoing medical issues.

Tuggeranong has been a great final placement for me. My time here has been tremendous. I love the congregation. They are very active and engaged. The people here are really committed and generous and willing to take risks and try new things. Let's face it, I came in with my fetid imagination in overdrive, and now the congregation has a big new mural on what was a blank external wall, new alliances with community groups like SeeChange, and some new regular activities, such as Christmas events. I got to develop intergenerational services with the congregation, and I could carry out some of my ecclesiastical fantasies with children, drama and craft activities as part of the service. I have enjoyed my time and it is a great congregation and was sad leaving it.

The future after Tuggeranong involves lots of medical appointments as we had trouble fitting them all in our last year. The future holds rest, moving to Dungog, a little village in the Hunter Valley. It is big enough not to be claustrophobic and has a tourist trade, a recently opened bike track and sustainability groups, cafés and brewery. We will be twenty minutes away from my brother, whom I am very close to, and an hour from Newcastle where other family live. The local church is considered to be one of the few live spots in the Hunter Valley so I am looking forward to being involved there. John and I have already been approached by the Hunter Presbytery to do stuff for them, but we want to have a good year off. We want to settle into our new house, do the garden and have a bit of a rest, then think about what we will do. I want to resume my hobbies such as family tree history research. When I was in Canberra in 2016, I did a diploma in Family History and this has fired up my interest again.

While in Wauchope, I completed a second Master's degree in Social Ecology which is about transition, learning how to transition communities, developing leadership skills and helping communities cope with change. My interim ministry placements led me into it. I finished the degree while in Wauchope and took these skills to WA. Tuggeranong has had the full benefit of them, learning about tipping points and working with community and people. I like a leadership style on a level playing field. While I am bossy and I push people to try new things, I also feel leadership is about walking alongside people and helping them find their own vision and ministry. I am good at process and developing ways of doing new things so I just don't sit there and tell people what to do. We work together.

So all in all it has been an unusual ministry path, and finishing at Tuggeranong has been a very affirming and satisfying end to it.

8

QUESTIONING WHO I AM

I have always had a sense of God but still question who I am and what are my gifts.

My name is Fran and I'm fairly new to Tuggeranong Uniting Church, TUC, having moved to Canberra from Sydney in July 2023. Thank you for being so welcoming. Michael and I had bought a house here some years ago which our family was minding (and rescuing) and had intended to retire here. However, Michael was offered a new job in chaplaincy in Canberra, this time in aged care, having come from mental health hospital chaplaincy, so a new chapter has begun for both of us.

I think I have always had a sense of God. I went to the local Anglican Sunday School and youth group in Chatswood with friends, but it wasn't until my late teens that I realised Jesus was an alive personal friend. I later shared a house for some years with a group of friends who had a strong desire to bring God's kingdom here on earth through ecumenical youthwork, media, social justice action and other creative Christian ministries. Though still working at the local library, I was influenced by this community to see a dynamic picture of God and the Christian community and when I married Michael from our local church (those were the days!), we felt we were on this journey together.

For many years while he was a youth worker with a mission organisation, we studied and travelled to various projects including Hornsby in Sydney, a farm at Peak Hill in the central west of NSW, ultimately spending almost 20 years in Tasmania, where Michael managed youth work projects and related accountancy, community radio, both in Launceston and a rehabilitation village in Poatina. I worked in casual roles in Launceston library and several schools as teaching support and helped with various projects.

Along the way and in different towns we had three lovely children who despite now living in major cities had a very rural background. (We don't deliver babies here" said the community hospital at Peak Hill when it was obvious we wouldn't make it to Parkes. Staff managed very well!)

Our time in Tasmania ended abruptly after revealing abuse in our organisation and finally, we returned to Sydney to lick our wounds and start again. After 30 years we were both faced with the questions through our mental exhaustion of: Who am I and, how can I find work? This began a process of slowly rediscovering myself, and a God of love and acceptance.

God graciously provided us with a caring local church and work. Hilariously I was offered casual work at my old Chatswood library (it had been more than 20 years!) To my delight I was able to do some children's work again as they had some staff gaps. Storytimes are so much fun, and Michael found a social work job running a program for the carers of the mentally ill at Kirribilli. It was lovely also to be back in Sydney to spend time with my elderly mum who died a few years ago at the age of 102.

We moved many times due to the fickle rental market, but each time found suitable accommodation for us and our student family who came and went (and came again.) During these years I discovered that I felt closest to God when things seemed totally out of my control.

I still question "who am I, what are my gifts and (sometimes) realise perhaps I'm afraid to be still and listen. Having cancer has me asking those questions more, but conversely also being reminded to stop and listen to God. A few years ago, I had the incredibly encouraging experience of studying a mental health CPE (clinical pastoral education) based at Macquarie (psych) Hospital in Sydney. One of the main things I learnt from fellow students and patients was that what I can bring is myself. I am enough. It's God's Spirit in me that connects with others, (and I also receive from them.)

I often find meaning from children's picture books. They have succinct language often with profound messages for all ages. "Giraffes can't dance" by Giles Andreae (read on YouTube) is one such story. Gerald, the giraffe, having spindly legs can't dance like the other animals and is humiliated and ridiculed for this. Wise words from his friend, the cricket who tells Gerald that we all can dance "When we find the music that we love."

Gerald needs his own music...

Listen to the swaying grass

And listen to the trees

To me the sweetest music

Is those branches in the trees.

So imagine that lovely moon

Is playing just for you

Everything makes music

If you really want it to."

I have renamed this story "Giraffes CAN dance."

As I hear my song I can dance.

Similarly, Psalm 139 vs 13-14 *You created every part of me, you put me together in my mother's womb. I praise you because you are to be feared; all you do is strange and wonderful I know it with all my heart.*

9

FROM LITTLE THINGS BIG THINGS GROW

My name is Jenny. A litle over twenty years ago an idea seeded in my mind and wouldn't go away. The two previous years at our annual spring fair we had a preloved clothing table. Lots of good clothing was donated but we didn't sell it all and so the remaining clothing was re-donated to a Vinnies bin. The following year the same thing happened and we had good things left. This time when I bagged them up, I couldn't quite take them to the Vinnies bins and so they stayed in the storeroom for the next six months.

I would have to say that looking back it was one of those God prompts which usually led me to following up someone or stepping out to do something. If ignored it continued to play on my mind. I talked about the idea of setting up a small monthly op shop with a couple of women from church and they were keen to support the venture. I had rarely been in an op shop and had no retail experience, so why me. I worked full time and had many other church and community commitments so where was I going to find the time.

The next step was to send a letter of proposal to church council. Approval was given and so in July 2006 we were up and running in the church meeting room for our first Friday and Saturday morning openings. We had a group of six of us and set up a roster with two people on each morning. We bought a couple of racks, printed advertising flyers and we were off. Our missional aim was to connect with the community and raise some money for mission projects/needs. We had several government housing townhouse and unit blocks to one side of the church. We set up a coffee spot as it would an opportunity for non-church goers to come through our front door and check us out. We had information about the church and activities always available and a friendly face to talk to. Customers got to know some of our regular volunteers on the desk and there were many pastoral conversations.

Donations originally came from church folk, families and their friends. We had a monthly sorting morning. With the money raised we were able to support some of our church ministries such as Karralika Christmas gifts, postage for Love in a Shoebox, Funsew and girls brigade projects, Salem parent funeral support costs, local customer house fire support. Also further afield hearing of need through some of our congregation to support a nurse in Botswana, Indulkna aboriginal community with an indoor play gym, national disaster appeals, Uniting World Projects, and a Nepal Care house for teenagers.

Community engagement grew with regular customers and one January we had a pop-up shop for three days in the Erindale centre. Eva's homemade jams and pickles were very popular and customers would return just for the new jams and pickles. We gradually purchased more racks on wheels and had some very sturdy ones made for us by Ian. We needed more storage space and so began using the demountable at the side of the church building.

We started as a little op shop venture to raise money for mission but we were now beginning to think seriously about the amount of clothing waste and our theme became reducing, reusing and recycling with posters around the building. We had some great clothes being donated and we could give them a second life, resurrected clothing so to speak, and so began our sustainability/ environmental thinking. The verse that came to me and in our proposal to Church Council was from Micah 6:8...

What does the Lord require of you? To act justly, to love mercy and walk humbly with God.

Before we knew it, we had been doing it for ten years and now we knew what the Micah verse had in mind for us. We now had a registered name Red Dove, the red dove from our Uniting Church logo. We were looking into expansion and requested the use of the meeting room inside the church building for sorting and some storage. We began using the auditorium for sales days which required setting up and packing away and there began our team of muscly men who set up and pack up for us.

About this time a community garden was established through the vision of a couple of other congregation members and then along came our new minister Elizabeth who was PASSIONATE about sustainability and the impact of a whole lot of things that were not helping our planet. We had information sheets about living more sustainably. She facilitated connection with community groups and encouraged us to dream bigger. We now opened on a Thursday as well and the seniors' friendship group meeting in the neighbourhood centre, across the carpark, became regular shoppers.

Fortunately, by now I was heading towards retirement and only working part time. We had a great team (the coordinating team of 4), community volunteers and other regular church volunteers. The increased selling days to three a month certainly increased sales and gave us more time to sort and price. I had red t-shirts printed with the Micah 6:8 verse, which most of our volunteers wear and clearly indicating our missional values and motivation. We connected with See Change and they have used our foyer areas on a Saturday for SWAP-A-THONS which brought in new customers for us as well. See Change also became involved with our yearly spring fairs and we advertise their monthly Repair Cafés. We had several fashion parades with the Girls Brigade and we have RED Dove open on a Friday evening when the community food van is in our carpark. When we had the SLEEP BUS in our carpark, we made RED DOVE available for free clothing.

Conversations with customers are deeper and richer with a wonderful spirit of generosity and kindness. Recently a wheelchair bound regular customer donated her overseas Christmas ornament collection and wanted us to gift them to our customers. Another regular customer brought in a homemade lemon slice for us because she appreciated the work we put in and another made jams and pickles for us before moving interstate. There are times when I am just blindsided by our customers' thoughtfulness and generosity and I believe at every opening there is a glimpse of the light of Christ shining through what we are doing. Many now see the church as a friendly, inclusive, safe and supportive place in our community. We have a prayer candle box and there are times following a conversation with someone we offer a candle for them to light and pray with them.

Op shopping has become fashionable and some younger people particularly are very conscious of the environmental impact of dumping used clothing and they resist cheap on-line shopping. Red Dove is evolving from a necessity for low-income families to a lifestyle choice. We see daughters bringing their mothers to shop and customers reporting they are very happy with our pricing and their finds as well as the chance to shop in a more sustainable way.

Our free table and bric-a-brac table encourages good reuse of items and passing them on. We often have new items donated, that are just not being used and at the back of a cupboard. Some shoppers are looking out for clothing items to remodel and repurpose and years ago we sent jeans off to be repurposed into paper. We send old towels and strained sheets off to the animal shelter and our excess children's clothing to Roundabout.

Thanks to Facebook advertising over the last few years our customers come from near and far and once they come, often return. We have over a hundred customers coming through our church doors each month, some spending as little as $2 and some up to $50+. Many customers have become our best donators.

In the scheme of things our sustainability effort is small as nationwide over 220,000 tons of clothing is still going to landfill and this only decreased by 1% in 2024. We are trying to be more sustainable, we have a Lions spectacles recycling box, used stamp box that supports Uniting Mission in Sydney and some customers regularly bring in food for our community foodbank.

Not only do we sell clothing but we give it away. We have vouchers that go in our Foodbank bags and to residents from the local

Karralika Drug Rehabilitation program. We regularly supply City Uniting with men's clothing for homeless men in the city. We donate to Roundabout with children's clothing and some of our excess supply of clothing would go to the Koomari bins for their recycling/repurposing and employing people with a disability. We supply clothing for the Lions' school formals annual project and donate clothing for the regular swap-a-thons with SEE Change. Cloth bags for our foodbank, children's beanies, patchwork quilts and crocheted rugs have been made and donated by some of our church members and friends. Recently during the winter, we sent many large bags of warm clothing, blankets and shoes to Cootamundra for workers from Samoa recently employed at the meatworks. Over the last 18 months we have posted off to the Remote Aboriginal Op Shop project over 20 bags of 10 kg of clothing with each bag costing $22 to post. We have supported flood and fire appeals, Aboriginal Youth in Wauchope and our Relationships and Growth ministry, which currently has a strong community focus. Becoming involved with the Presbytery Op Shop support group on regular zoom meetings has given us lots of new ideas to support our small venture.

Some of our customers say "I have bought three things so I will donate three back, next time I come." We are trying in our small way at Red Dove to promote working for the good for our planet environmentally while supporting needs in our community and beyond.

Unbelievably from twenty years of our monthly openings, we have raised close to $150,000, no small thing, and all from clothing and goods people no longer need and have donated.

Red Dove has done a lot of good. It's dedicated to sustainability with affordable good quality clothing options particularly with cost of living pressures and caring for our community. By promoting the reuse of garments, we aim to reduce waste and encourage mindful consumption. We never imagined twenty years ago what two bags of clothing would start. Our storage demountable is very aged and has had several break-ins and each time repaired amazingly by some of our church men. We are now looking at a building extension for several uses. There is still more we could do? A huge thanks to all who have volunteered in so many ways along the way you have been an amazing blessing. What will the next ten years bring? We look forward to how this venture can continue to love and bless those in our community and shine the light of Christ through all we do and say.

10

INTO MY HEART

My name is Lorna. I was born in China, the third of six children and only girl. My parents were missionaries with the China Inland Mission (CIM) whose policy was not to impose imperialistic western ideas. They wore Chinese clothes, ate Chinese food and spoke Chinese.

My mother, Marjorie Ament had a very strong call to be a missionary. At the same time as she attended Melbourne Bible Institute, my father, Frederick 'Fred' Smith, was travelling around New South Wales with the evangelist Rev John Ridley, as well as studying with the NSW Baptist Theological College. In response to a call for young missionaries, my mother travelled to the Shanghai Headquarters of the CIM. She excelled in language study. While she was there, my father was also welcomed to the language school.

At the conclusion of her studies Marjorie was appointed to a station in Yunan Province not far from the southern border and Fred, a short time later, to Shensi Province in the mid north where he began a correspondence with Marjorie. It took a month for each letter to reach its destination, so Marjorie knew that she was engaged to be married one month before Fred. They met up again in Shanghai just three weeks before their wedding and a new life in Hanchung and other towns in Shensi Province not far from Sian, the capital, where the entombed warriors were later discovered.

Our family lived in a compound with other missionary families, various other buildings and a church and my father would trek to outlying villages to meet and talk with interested people. During a World War 2 Japanese air raid my father took my two older brothers down into a shelter. He had to leave the nurse and my mother in the house. My mother was well on the way to giving birth to me.

Ridley, my oldest brother by 4 years, went to boarding school in Jiadin in the west, away from the fighting. He then flew with Andrew, 2 years younger, to Kalimpong in India for safety. Ridley did not see our mother for two years, and then only briefly. The separation trauma affected him significantly. When the war ended both boys arrived in Shanghai where the CIM school was re-established and I, aged 6, joined them.

It was also the time for my parents' second furlough in Australia - the 18 months long holiday and deputation work. They could only afford to take my three younger brothers, Clifford and the twins, Ross and Donald. Our mother later said it was 'agony' - it 'nearly killed' her leaving the three older children behind. I was terrified, having never been separated from her in my life. My big brothers, I was told, would be there as well as 'Auntie Kathleen', a missionary from our station, who would be staying in Shanghai for some time.

I stood in the playground one day watching the other children playing. The whole world was grey. I cried myself to sleep every night for a long time. One night the headmaster's wife picked me up in her arms and carried me up and down the corridor until I fell asleep. Another night an older teacher took me to her room down the corridor where I lay gazing at the luminous hands of her clock for a long time. The school of over 100 children moved to what had been the American School in Kuling in the Lushan Mountains in central China. This became the CIM school for the children of missionaries and some foreign business people. Despite my acute homesickness I loved the beauty of these mountains.

After eighteen months our parents returned to China and our family was reunited for the summer holidays in Shanghai where our father had a temporary job looking after the office and shop. It was absolute heaven being all together and enjoying the swings and play equipment in the grounds.

But then it was time to go back to school in Kuling and the agony of separation. It was more than I could manage at that young age.

One day I found myself on the floor of our bathroom looking up at some very concerned adults. I had fitted and the explanation could only be the trauma of separation. Following this fit I spent three weeks in hospital before going back to school where I had to repeat a year!

Our parents visited the school a couple of times, staying nearby during the holidays, but then, of course, they had to return to Hanchung. I was always homesick, resulting in two more fits, and I spent time recuperating in the school's 'Sick Bay' where the patients were all treated with great kindness. This was where I was introduced to a delectable spread called 'Vegemite' which, I was told, was plentiful in Australia! I made friends with another lonely girl in my class and played with the presents sent from my Grandma and Auntie Muriel, including a koala who I named 'Paddy-Paws'.

When my special little brother Clifford joined the school, I was overjoyed because now I had a purpose - to look after him. During a summer holiday at the Children's Special Service Mission, we sat on the floor in the gymnasium singing choruses. As we sang 'Into my heart, into my heart, come into my heart, Lord Jesus' this became my prayer and I was assured that I was now a Christian. Clifford also decided then and there to become a Christian. Many years later he assured me that this was the start of his spiritual journey.

All four of our family were at last going home to Hanchung for Christmas 1950! The teachers told us to take with us our most precious possessions because we might not be returning. I was delirious with the prospect! Experiencing a most wonderful family time, we had until mid-April when the local authorities issued visas to us and the remaining single missionaries to travel by train to the border and out to Hong Kong.

After a short holiday in Hong Kong we boarded the Carthage passenger liner to Singapore and then the Gorgon freighter down the west coast of Australia to Fremantle. There we changed to the Indian Pacific train and so right across Australia to Sydney. It was wonderful being hugged by our relatives in Sydney. We caught the train three weeks later to Blackheath in the Blue Mountains where our father had accepted a call to be Minister of the Baptist Church. Our parents could have moved to another country for extended missionary service, but they made the wise decision to settle where all our family could be together as we made our way through the challenges of our education journeys.

I was filled with happiness during five and a half years in Blackheath where we were all together. Neighbours later commented that they often heard laughter spilling out of our windows. We younger children walked to Blackheath Primary School, later catching the train to Katoomba High School which Ridley and Andrew attended. We rode our bikes all over Blackheath. I began to sing solos in church and sometimes sang with Clifford who had an exceptionally beautiful soprano voice; more beautiful than many of the recordings of boy sopranos we heard on the ABC!

I enjoyed the high school choir, some acting and singing roles, winning prizes for verse speaking and prose reading, and coming first in my class. I looked forward to being a prefect one day until we were told that we would be moving to Sydney where our father had accepted a call to Pymble Baptist Church.

I attended Hornsby Girls' High School where, to my surprise, after only one year I was elected a prefect and then Head Prefect! One of nine students, I represented all the girls' public high schools of NSW, when we were presented to the Queen Mother on her visit to an enormous schools' assembly in the Sydney Showground. After my unexpectedly huge year, which included the Leaving Certificate, I spent two years at Balmain Teachers College and three years teaching at Lidcombe Primary School in western Sydney.

I was in love with Rex Orr all through these years and, while he completed a four-year course at the Baptist Theological College, I studied there for two years until, at the end of this period of waiting, we were at last married. He decided not to be ordained and, instead, we travelled to Point Pearce Aboriginal Reserve in South Australia where we started a family. Rex was in charge of all the office administration for four years before obtaining the position of

Superintendent of Koonibba Aboriginal Reserve west of Ceduna. We lived there for five years, enjoying our four children and the friends we made in Ceduna, and performing in music productions and choral performances which Rex organised and conducted.

Rex was always community minded and he aimed to be the last superintendent on Koonibba Aboriginal Reserve. He encouraged and promoted leadership, self-sufficiency and organisation by the First Nations peoples living there. I supported him in this while we raised our four young children, Roxie, Bronwyn, Elliott and Charmian. They were busy times.

We moved to Adelaide where Rex studied social work. I began wonderful singing lessons with Donald Munro at the Conservatorium. I enjoyed performing solos there and in other venues, including the soprano leads over several years in Gilbert and Sullivan Society productions. I sang in several choirs and was invited to join The Corinthian Singers. Eventually this led to busking in Rundle Mall in period costume, a role for which I became well-known and was persuaded to sing on 'New Faces'.

In 1975 Rex and George Smith, his best friend, discovered a huge house for sale in Mt Barker in the Adelaide Hills which had been the Methodist Rest Home - 'Auchendarroch' was reborn. It became our home for eight years, along with four other families and other people living in the community. We enjoyed the grounds and gardens which offered the chance for Rex to organise and bring the local community together for carols by candlelight across a number of years.

When we moved to Adelaide and the Adelaide hills, we initially attended Flinders Street Baptist Church. It was there that I made a record of sacred songs. We were later invited to Pilgrim Uniting Church where we joined a group of musicians learning the songs of pianist and composer Douglas Simper. I had been performing in a number of concerts and eisteddfods with a couple of pianists, but now here was someone truly impressive! I asked him if he would be willing to be my accompanist and he simply said, "All right." We worked together professionally for two years performing in concerts and shows and playing and singing for church services. Rex managed many of our events.

The Orrs, Rex and myself and our children, and the Simpers, Doug and Gail with their children, Michelle and Damien, became good friends, visiting each other and sharing meals in our homes. This was a period of joyful shows, concerts and performances across many venues, including the Auchendarroch Christmas Carols. Michelle was often the page turner for Douglas's playing, and she and Charmian were my costume change assistants for many performances.

Times and relationships changed. We moved from Auchendarroch to Adelaide. Through complex and difficult experiences, I left my marriage to live with Doug, after he and Gail had separated. Rex and Gail lived together and later married.

During 1987 I visited Sydney every weekend as' 'Old Sydney's Singing Sensation' at the Old Sydney Parkroyal Hotel in The Rocks. Doug and I moved to Sydney with our children, Charmian and Damien. We worshipped at Pitt Street Uniting Church and were married by Rev Dorothy McRae McMahon in 1989. Our wedding was the morning service where our children took part, leading prayers, readings, and singing.

When the Old Sydney Park Royal changed hands, my singing position finished abruptly. The recession hit and there was little work for musicians. I joined the Marketing Department of Sydney City Mission/Mission Australia and, for ten years, I visited supporters and spoke at clubs, community groups and churches around Sydney, always including singing in my talks. 'Douglas', now using the name that had been my favourite since I was a child, decided to do further study, achieving a distinction in Master's in Creative Arts and a scholarship to do a PhD in Music Composition. While he studied and composed, he was Director of Music in Parramatta and Gordon Uniting Churches. He also volunteered with Sydney City Mission, organising two concerts in Sydney Town Hall.

After gaining his Ph.D. with the dissertation and music theatre work, 'Venus in Eritrea', Douglas searched for academic positions overseas. They were scarce and he settled for Head of Department in a high school in Birmingham, U.K. Our children were all independent so off we went on this new adventure in 2001! The school turned out to be just like the film 'To Sir With Love'! Douglas, with all his experience and expertise, lasted just one term.

Soon after Douglas took up a position as Director of Music and organist at 'Priory Place Methodist Church' in the centre of Doncaster. He delighted the more youthful and enthusiastic members with initiating new programs using their grand piano, previously used only for concerts, and other instruments including drums. This was despite the growing anger of the senior fraternity who wished to get rid of him and his 'unconventional' approach - and finally did! We lived in Doncaster for eighteen months, making some wonderful lifelong friends, and I drove to Scunthorpe Methodist to assist half-time for a year in their drop-in centre.

We heard about a marvellous school music service, Somerset Music, attended an interview day as 'The Aussie Minstrels', along with six other performing musicians, and were accepted. However, we subsequently discovered that all of us were accepted simply to be displayed in a file that schools could examine to make their own choices. Despite this, we moved to Shepton Mallet in Somerset, the base from which Douglas would travel to a number of towns to teach individual piano lessons in high schools. After our first meagre Christmas I worked for three months half-time at a factory packaging their desserts! I then worked part-time for Somerset Wildlife Trust until we set up a piano and singing school in the Shepton Mallet Baptist Church. This continued successfully with very much appreciated student concerts until we left England.

In Somerset, we lived at Litton in the Mendip Hills, followed by Midsomer Norton south of beautiful Bath. The Methodist Chapel in Oakhill Village became our spiritual home and Douglas played the organ for some time at Cheddar Methodist Church and Litton Anglican Church. He also led the music once a month at a family service in St Stephens Anglican Church in Bath. Occasionally we gave ourselves the treat of visiting Wells Cathedral where worship led by their official clergy team was moving and stimulating. We enjoyed friendships in all these charming places.

During our fifteen years in England various family members came to see us and we visited our children's families in the Antipodes six times, on one occasion staying ten days with each family. We were delighted to attend Bronwyn's wedding in France and to provide the music for the wedding of their new family friends in a village near Lyon. We stayed en route with Charmian and her family in Hong Kong during our journeys.

After Bronwyn and Charmian visited us in England in 2016, Charmian confided that she was dealing with cancer. She invited me to come with her for a week to a holiday healing centre in Thailand. Despite all her efforts, the cancer advanced and we decided it was time to return to Australia to be near where she was receiving treatment. Douglas organised a memorable farewell concert in St Luke's Church in Bath for ourselves and our outstanding piano and singing students. Damien joined us from Copenhagen, where he was living with his family, and sang in the choir for the service. We returned to Sydney where we spent some months visiting Charmian in a hospice before she died in November 2016.

We were introduced to beautiful Tathra on the Far South Coast on a trip with Bronwyn who had just purchased a café, 'Blend'. Sydney's rents were too expensive for us so on our second visit we saw an impressive home to rent on a hill at Wapengo on the road north from Tathra to Bermagui. We put in an application and were successful. We enjoyed a lovely time living there. It was a really spiritual place on Yuin country.

We had a ceremony bringing family and friends together to walk on Yuin country, circle a magnificent gum tree, and plant a tree in memory of Charmian. Elliott, my son, like his father, brings music to community and community together. With the beat of the djembe, Elliott has played at many significant family events, including for his younger sister Charmian's wedding. He played djembe at the memorial ceremony for Charmian while a tree of remembrance was planted.

Living on the New South Wales coast from the end of 2016 to 2023 was a rewarding and relaxing period of 'winding down'. I painted many paintings of the beautiful local scenery and Douglas enjoyed teaching his piano method to many appreciative students. We had visits from family, concerts, and dinners in our large, but draughty home. We had the daily enjoyment of Bronnie's cafe and, later on, the restaurant, 'Pividori's', which Bronnie and her wonderful Troy revamped impressively. Douglas's music oversight, including the 'Bega Big Sing' at St John's in Bega was followed by involvement in the lively, welcoming group at Tathra Uniting Church. I enjoyed conducting the Tathra Singers and Douglas enjoyed accompanying.

Bushfire scares finally prompted us to move from the winding road through Wapengo into Tathra where we rented a unit with a balcony, the home for six permanently flowering yellow and rose crucifix orchids. In a nearby small children's park friends and family came to replant a jacaranda tree in memory of Charmian. Kind friends tended the garden for Charmian's tree and we felt embraced and appreciated in the Tathra community. Christmas carols and sing alongs were lovely community events, also enjoyed by those passing through in the Christmas holidays.

In 2008 Douglas had double bypass heart surgery in England. I was grateful for my eldest daughter, Roxie's return to England at that time. She was able to take care of Douglas and myself while going through that difficult period. Since then, Douglas's health has been excellent. Now, as we indulged in walks on the Tathra Beach and coffee with friends, we began to notice his feet shuffling and the need for care to avoid falls. He was diagnosed with Progressive Supranuclear Palsy, a rare disease for which there is no treatment. His muscles weakened, he needed to be careful when he was swallowing food and his body became thin. It was devastating to see these changes but through it all, Douglas has kept his focus and continues to surprise us with his capacity to play the piano.

One night in November 2023 Douglas could not endure the pain in his jaw and begged to be taken to Bega Hospital. A week later he was transported by ambulance to 'Mirinjani', an excellent Uniting Aged Care home in Canberra. He has received very good care at Mirinjani, and while this has been a difficult time of transition for us both, I am very grateful to be in one of the best places we can be, surrounded by such care. We are not far from Bronnie and Troy who, with visiting family members and friends, always make us feel loved. I have celebrated my 85th birthday with style and the loving kindness of Douglas and my family around me.

Canberra is a beautiful surprise. Music continues with some playing and singing, and we have found a spiritual home in the open arms of Tuggeranong Uniting Church.

(With thanks for some editing input from Lorna's daughter, Roxie.)

11

A CALL TO MISSION

the Uniting Church Stamp Committee

My name is Lorraine. It's amazing where a small coloured square of paper on an envelope may lead! Stamp collecting, something that was of no interest to me as a child, led to an abiding interest, even an obsession. My husband, a collector for many years, asked me to help him out sorting some of his stamps into an album – and I was hooked, enthusiastic – even obsessive at times. A personal 'hobby' that gave pleasure continued for many years.

We moved from Gunnedah to Canberra, and at a Presbytery meeting the retiring Stamp Co-ordinator, for this Presbytery, was looking for someone to take over the role. I was challenged to volunteer, without really knowing what it involved. It was like being thrown into the deep end of a river! However, the more I thought about it I realised that this was more than just filling in a role, it was a call to mission.

Initially it involved collecting the stamps from Presbytery meetings – quite a daunting task. For a while a small group gathered at Wesley to trim and sort, but age and circumstances changed, so I began to work from home. Using a spare bedroom as a Stamp Room in our former home didn't involve moving everything to another room. But life in a retirement village meant re-organising available space, which at times can be frustrating but the end result always rewarding. But times change and now I only collect from Tuggeranong and Wesley Churches. It's either a feast or a famine; sometimes there are large bags, albums or just a few tucked in a large envelope. Yet I still find pleasure in performing the task and continue to recognise that this a calling. These little pieces of coloured paper are sent to The Stamp Committee based in Sydney to raise funds to assist parishes with important projects.

The Stamp Committee was started in 1977 when the Uniting Church in Australia was formed. The Committee comprises of volunteers whose sole aim is to raise funds to support the work of the Uniting Church. Volunteers from churches all over NSW and the ACT contribute to this ministry by collecting and donating stamps (and occasionally whole collections) to the Stamp Committee. The donated stamps and collections are sold to dealers to raise funds. The Committee also puts together books of stamps to sell to collectors. Since 1977 the Committee has raised over $900,000. Annually there is an application process for grants advertised with amounts generally up to $1000.

Applications are made through the Committee for a wide diversity of need in church communities as well as outreach in the community including

- Healthy breakfasts for school children
- Equipment for community kitchens and gardens
- Serving meals for the homeless
- Supporting people with disabilities with job skills
- Providing recording systems for worship for rural communities
- Creating support for older people to have confidence with modern technology
- Outreach and support for women suffering health issues to meet together to make Wrap with Love Quilts.
- Refurbishing and assisting new op shops
- Purchasing equipment to repair, restore and renew items instead of going into landfill

In Sydney the stamps are sold, mostly to dealers and collectors. Even with the convenience of E-mails, stamps continue to raise money! It's amazing what that humble piece of paper can achieve:

The challenge is to continue Saving Our Stamps so this ministry can continue.

12

SPIRITUALITY AND MY STORY

The rich tapestry of God's enduring presence in my life

[Louise's spirituality story is the last chapter of a resource "Illness, Recovery and Wellbeing." She wrote it a few years ago in her work as a psychologist after her own cancer experience. She has added a POSTSCRIPT to that chapter following my invitation for her story to be included in this book.]

My name is Louise and part of my recovery, the part that emerged in the washup of cancer, about a year after the initial drama, was making sense of my spiritual story. As I began to read more into the research about resilience and recovery, I came across material that suggested tracing ones' spiritual history is very helpful in the process of healing. Kenneth Pargament, in his book "The Psychology of Religion and Coping" talks about the religious practices that can support recovery from Post Traumatic Stress Disorder (PTSD). Pargament and other authors in this space, discuss how therapy and spirituality can complement each other in the process. One of the therapeutic tasks that comes from this research, is to write a personal spiritual autobiography.

For most of my life, I have been a questioner and doubter; it is as much a part of me as the colour of my eyes. We evolve our understandings of many aspects of life as we grow older. Politics, scientific theories, economic theories, our psychological theories of being human, have all evolved and been updated along the way. It is part of human development. So why would it be any different with faith? Why is a faith that is stuck in a childhood acquired version any more loyal to the cause, than one that has gone through several iterations? Both Richard Rohr and Brian McLaren assert that it is certainty that is the opposite of faith, not doubt. Julia Baird says this about doubt: "Just as courage is persisting in the face of fear, so is faith in the presence of doubt."

For some, who have faith or a set of religiously based beliefs, it seems very easy to not question them. For others it is much more logical and sometimes even safer to take a position of nonbelief and steer clear of institutional religion altogether. What can be difficult, is to stay the course, to continue to question and become comfortable with the experience of doubt. For me, this was the only way I could get to a deeper understanding of my inherited beliefs; and for it to evolve to an enduring faith. In the end, I have chosen to continue to question and disrupt the status quo whilst staying connected to my faith as a Christian. Historically Christian beliefs have been exploited and hijacked; they have been associated over time with some truly abhorrent events. I have wondered many times; do I give up on it completely? I can hear some voices right now yelling yes. For me though, despite these limitations and long periods of my own non-engagement with formalised religious organisations, I continue to identify with Christianity. However, not the version of religion I grew up with.

There are versions of Christianity and images of God that I can no longer inadvertently or misguidedly support. White Christian supremacy, literalist Christianity that rejects advances in science and many other disciplines, punishment-based Christianity, as well as positions on sexuality that practice exclusion, all fall short of what I believe the essence the Jesus' message was about. Faith appears to be a universal phenomenon that has evolved over many thousands of years; and is still evolving. God however described, has been there throughout evolution. The person of Jesus who historically lived two thousand years ago, who we meet in the scriptures, for me, is the human embodiment of a God who is loving and inclusive. Interpreting ancient and sacred scriptures means we understand that they were written in a particular context, with a particular view of what it meant to be human.

Like evolution, it is important to understand that revelation is a work in progress; and that our contemporary faith questions about what it means to be human deserve legitimate enquiry and consideration; in relation to where our understanding of humanity is up to now.

Several years ago, I came across the work of Robert Grant, a psychologist who had worked for many years in the area of severe trauma. His work had a great influence on how I stayed well when working with child protection cases. The worst of what we can imagine was happening to the children, and in the families, I was working with. At the time I was losing the ability to see good in people. I was working with so much wrongdoing. I participated in some training with Grant who quoted a line of scripture from the Gospel of Matthew (10:16); "Behold, I am sending you out as sheep in the midst of wolves, so be wise as serpents and innocent as doves." I pondered these words many times during my years working as a psychologist; and this act of contemplation enabled me to stay connected to the purpose of my work. I believe it was instrumental in managing the damaging impact of working in child protection.

As I worked my way into recovery after breast cancer I came back to his work on spirituality and trauma in a book called "The Way of the Wound". In this, Grant talks about spirituality as the need to directly experience the Spirit. To live in a connected relationship with creation. Like others he also proposes that it is spirituality, in particular, that leads us to wholeness. He suggests that spirituality, initially is a way of knowing; and that over time gradually becomes a way of being. Looking at spirituality this way might explain the enduring nature of my doubt filled faith.

To engage with questions of spirituality, often what is required, is a re-examination of ideas that one might have grown up with as well as images of God that do not hold up under scrutiny. Fr Richard Rohr contends, that for most people, their childhood acquired Christian faith equates intellectually with our understanding of Father Christmas. In this he does not blame or judge anyone, just acknowledges that the way Christianity is communicated is intellectually very limited. If we are to align ourselves with some form of belief that belief must hold up under intellectual scrutiny, and particularly so in times of crisis.

There is a theme park in Orlando Florida called the 'Holy Land Experience'. Christians and many others go there to see the Jesus story re-enacted and taught. People watch the re-enactments of the Crucifixion and Resurrection story to name just a couple, with a heartfelt emotional response. Christian actors who work there, when interviewed about their faith, share strongly held beliefs about the story and its meaning to them. The way the Jesus story is recounted in this theme park is indicative of a literal view of the Hebrew and Christian Scriptures. This theme park would appeal to many Christian faithfuls who read Christian scriptures in the same way they read historical accounts of the Second World War. However, this approach presents difficulties, particularly when we face situations that are distressing and out of our control.

The way we are taught about Christianity, and I think this would also apply to other religions, is in a developmentally childlike way. For many of us, learning about God, and in my case Jesus, started when I was very little. We know that small children learn about the world through concrete and literal ways; and often have a magical understanding of how things work. Children readily accept the more fantastical stories in scripture; as well as other cultural stories such as Santa Claus, the Easter Bunny and the Tooth Fairy. The trouble is that religion, often falls prey, to the same process of discarded beliefs that apply to the Tooth Fairy. Literalist or fundamentalist understandings of scripture exacerbate this. If we could understand that sacred scriptures and writings are not written primarily as historical accounts and can cope with this idea, then their influence and deeper theological meanings can help our faith evolve. Churches have a long way to go in helping people cultivate age-appropriate images of God; and a theological approach to understanding scripture that is more evolved. This problem, however, is not a one-way street. Many academically trained pastors and ministers lead lives of quiet desperation because their congregations resist preaching and teaching that stretches them beyond their understandings of biblical interpretation and faith.

This tension can lead to a somewhat magical understanding of God, and Jesus, (in the Christian context;) that will not stand test of time when trauma and tragedy bulldoze their way into our lives. If there is a God of miracles, we might wonder why there were millions of Jewish believers during the Holocaust who were not saved. At the same time, we might also wonder why that for those who did survive, they claimed it as a miracle of God? Does this mean that God might have favourites?

Illness is another flashpoint when it comes to this God of miracles. I remember the parish priest at the church I was attending many years ago, like many Christian pilgrims, travelled to Lourdes in the south of France, to pray for a cure for his lung cancer. A short period of time later, he died. Again, here is the question of miracle cures and tragic deaths. If we are sick, or in distress what do we pray for and how do we do it? What can we expect when we pray? If the outcome of our situation is dire; and not a hoped-for cure then how do we understand the action of God? Again, drawing on the work of Brian McLaren he suggests that there is a restricted intellectualism in Christianity; inadvertently acting as interference in coming to terms with such pressing questions. He quotes Dr Darren Slade:

"When we go around saying '...that miracles happen a lot,' we are opening the door for charlatans to come in and swindle desperate people. We prime people to get duped and get hurt."

These are the real-life dilemmas posed for people who profess a faith. People who are raised with a set of beliefs that intellectually don't hold up when tough times arrive. When disaster, catastrophe or illness does strike it is not unusual to experience a disruption in faith and at the heart of the crisis discover a deeply rooted sense of doubt. What can be troubling to identify is that this disrupted faith may just be about childhood understandings being shed, making space for a more nuanced and comprehensive spirituality. Faith can be very hard won, and if it is lost in the process of a crisis, it is sad to think it is no longer there enriching our minds and hearts, as we make our way through the toughest experiences of our lives. This is partly my story as I was recovering from breast cancer.

As a young adult, and well into my 30's and 40's, I professed a strong belief in the Christian message. I identified as a card-carrying member of my church. I would probably be described as a progressive lefty Christian by some; and a socially conservative Christian by others. In my thirties, I disengaged from the Catholic church as I was tired of its stuck and sexist ways. I joined the home church movement. As I said to my husband at the time, "I am sick of watching men prance around altars in dresses whilst at the same time being female meant one had very little voice in the vision and direction of the institution." I then participated in a home church group for about ten years, and some of the members remain my friends. That group then folded and up until recently, I have not belonged to any church; but interestingly my spirituality has continued to blossom.

I was fortunate in my first degree to be able to study a major in theology; and this initially helped me form what I would call a more evolved understanding of the Christian message. What I took away from that study was an understanding that there were many contradictions in accounts retold in scripture; that these scriptures were written as theological and mythical (not fairy-tale) truths; and to read these accounts in a literal way was to misinterpret them. I was also taught that the historical evidence was strong supporting the idea that Jesus did walk this earth. While there were differences in the four gospels; some of the accounts of his life that appeared in all four of them, added to the likelihood these events did occur.

I found this quite helpful but years later I found myself still wondering about what did happen; and in a sense, I have gone through a deconstruction of my inherited beliefs. When we think about how we reconstruct our own stories of events in our lives; and the interpretation we bring to them it is not unusual that context and embellishment, along with insight and hindsight, characterise our life narratives.

Similarly, the stories in scripture were passed down through oral tradition and by the time they were recorded in writing the authors were bringing to life accounts of events passed down through a range of recollections, interpretations, different lenses of theology and the context of the time. The task for us is to understand the literary style, the theological emphasis, and the cultural context of them, and then it is possible to decipher to a degree the truth or wisdom that is within them.

To understand the scriptures that are the basis of Christianity as sources of theological and mythical truth, rather than just historical events is to enter a world of controversy. The problem is that this very word, myth, has been devalued. These days the word is used to convey the idea of a lie, or a misrepresentation that is being used to manipulate the truth. This is completely contrary to the approach of the original authors, who used this literary style to convey eloquently, the wisdom and truth of their faith as far as they understood it in ancient times. Myths are now often regarded as irrelevant or as non-scientific rubbish. When it dawns on us that the scriptures are a mix of an oral tradition, and literary style, as well as theological emphasis, it is easy to see how for some people, this represents a complete loss of faith. For me it represented a loss of my childhood acquired beliefs.

Surprisingly, this controversy has also helped to reignite and enrich my faith, as it has helped to leach out any of the magical traces of my early understandings of God. There is a mystical, but not magical divine presence in my life. As time has gone on, my understanding of scripture has evolved; and ironically it has made it more interesting and relevant. Strangely enough, understanding the divergent and contentious views on sacred scriptures across different theological schools and churches, opens up a place for people like me where these differences can co-exist. If more people understood the divergent and contested views in the broad church of Christianity; more people may legitimately find a place within it. There is a place for doubters and questioners like me in religious tradition, you just have to find the places where uncertainty and questioning is valued.

"Our differences are treasures and they're also tools. They are useful, valid, worthy, and important to share. Recognising this, not only in ourselves but in the people around us, we begin to rewrite more and more stories of not mattering. We start to change the paradigms around who belongs, creating more space for more people. Step by step, we can lessen the loneliness of not belonging......It remains a damming fact of life that we ask too much of those who are marginalised and too little of those who are not." Michelle Obama (The Light We Carry)

For me, faith is the reality I perceive as God endures. Like a heritage rose bush that has had years of tenderness and care, along with long periods of neglect, it continues to bloom year after year. Importantly, my faith no longer rests on whoever of these theologians or scripture scholars is "right", it is the deeper more mystical dimensions of spirituality, not a particular set of beliefs that is the foundation of my faith. As a progressive, inclusive, and interfaith (and some would say dangerous) believer, I am less prone to thinking that I don't measure up in my identity as a Christian. I am no longer interested in the arrogant certainty displayed by some versions of Christianity nor the derision from some quarters of atheism. I love the enormity of the divine mystery and the poetry of a life lived with soul. Mary Oliver, the American poet expresses this well:

I have refused to live
locked in the orderly house of reasons and proofs.
The world I live in and believe in
is wider than that. And anyway, what's wrong with Maybe?
You wouldn't believe what once or twice I have seen.
I'll just tell you this:
only if there are angels in your head will you
ever, possibly, see one.

In his book *Soil*, Matthew Evans writes that it is the underground economy of microbes and worms and wriggly things in soil that enables plants to grow. It is the complex life of soil, a living, breathing network of hidden life that feeds, and feeds off the roots of plants which produces the food we eat. He contends the science is now indicating this underground life of soil, not fertilizer, as was once thought, supports the life of plants. Life, Evans says, begets life. Tim Costello in his book on 'Faith' alludes to something similar, when it comes to faith. He says:

the naturalist view that exerts existence comes from nonexistence simply makes no sense.

How does existence come from non-existence he asks, or being from nonbeing? Costello's question parallels what Evans talks about. The idea of life begetting life is a helpful analogy for me, for how we might understand the existence of God. Costello questions the atheists and physicists who suggest that it is magical to think that life in the cosmos originally came from life. He contends that is just as magical to believe that life comes from non-life. We don't understand the mystery of existence, but strangely gardening gives me a sense of it.

What is difficult for many people these days is the idea of aligning oneself to a belief system, or a religious organisation which may have a troubling history, and presence in the world. To identify as Christian today is to acknowledge the whole dirty history of Christianity, in conjunction with its liberating message. For me, doing the whole Christian thing without some people to hang out with is difficult, keeping skin in the game is not easy. I have not wanted to discard my Christian heritage or lose my faith, but to do so has meant a major rethink and a journey along a solitary path.

Julia Baird writes in her book Phosphorescence:

If I could advise church leaders, I would tell them to stop lecturing about sin, relax their defensive crouch and just listen, for a decade, or a century. ....The damage of the child sex abuse scandals and revelations of hidden domestic violence in faith communities has caused a deep and rational cynicism about the church, as have the intolerance of and ignorance about the LGBTQI community and complicity in the colonisation and exclusion of Indigenous people. Leaders have been at best, slow to understand that the church must be a sanctuary for the abused not a refuge for the abuser..... It is not easy, especially for women, or members of the LGBTQI community, to maintain something resembling faith in the midst of ugly politicking and hateful sentiments. It makes belief seem hateful and oppressive.

Contemplating and understanding the action of God in our world, and with illness in particular is another aspect of faith's puzzling mystery. If the divine is a reality, exactly what do we believe about it? Beliefs about the action of God in the world will vary widely along a continuum, from an omnipotent being who responds to those who earnestly pray for and receive God's action; in precisely the way they have asked for it; to a simple yearning to experience a sense of presence or peace. Many have grown up with the belief that if they pray earnestly enough, or hard enough, or for exactly the right thing, then their prayers will be answered. Unfortunately, with this type of thinking we may conclude that those who are cured are blessed, and those who are in pain or remain ill are not. To me this type of thinking about God just does not make sense.

If we do believe in a God of action what does a Godlike intervention mean and look like in this world. A highly relevant question when we are ill. Let's first look at the way other unusual things can happen in the world. A good example of this is the placebo effect. This effect is a phenomenon expected when the efficacy of drugs is being assessed in clinical trials. It is a well-established and well-known fact, that in any given study of any given drug, about 30% of those taking the placebo drug (an inert substance that they think is the drug under investigation), will report the same health benefits expected by the drug itself. In the case of medications used for menopausal symptoms, the placebo effect can be reported as up to 50% of a participant sample. Now think about when Jesus was reported to have said to a woman healed of persistent bleeding; (Luke 8: 43-48) that her faith had made her whole. What happened then, and what was the deeper message in this story? Was this something like the placebo effect? We don't really know, but what we do know is that faith in something is not exclusive to the domain of religion. People can have faith in many things and that faith can move mountains. As

Albert Einstein is supposed to have said: *There are only two ways to live your life; one is as though nothing is a miracle. The other is as though everything is a miracle.*

Sarah Bachelard – the minister of the church that I now attend (via Zoom) has preached on this story in the Gospel. Here is snippet of her take on it:

I've argued that God (as conceived in the Christian tradition) does not interrupt the life of the world from the outside – does not act through a series of interventions on demand. If we think of God like this, then God becomes nothing more than a bigger version of us, and divine action becomes reactive to circumstance. But, in Christian understanding, God is not (like us) an actor among actors, negotiating with an environment. God simply is the ever-present mercy and love on which all life depends, and God's being and act are one.

The various healing stories in the gospels suggests breakthrough. When I think about the miracle of my life and my recovery, I think this idea of breakthrough resonates. Science and technology that has moved to a point where the illnesses that I have suffered have been curable, or at least manageable. At a different point of history, the miracle will be different again. As human endeavour continues to work more medical miracles for me it signals the quiet but never-ending presence of the divine in history. Remember Matthew Evens the soil man, and his thinking about life begetting life. For me, every life that has been devoted to progressing science and technology, is a life that has enabled my life to continue. This for me is the miracle of life begetting life.

However, the question of faith and the relentless incidence of incurable and or terminal illness remains. Again, I will share Sarah's words:

So let me just offer this. It seems to me that faith is fundamentally about radical entrustment – entrusting myself, entrusting those I love to God, undefendedly and beyond pretence at self-sufficiency. To do this, we must trust that God wills our good – our growth, liberation, reconciliation and fullness of life – and I believe God does. But exactly how this good manifests in particular lives at particular times, how it breaks through the risks and limits of this world, how it changes or transforms our circumstances – well, this isn't something whose form we're guaranteed. Faith is simply the choice, the stubborn willingness to stay open before God, as best we can, and come what may.

In the end my sense of it is that God is and wants to be in the thick of it with us. The only thing that separates us from this sense of presence is our thinking about it. Maybe we need to go easy on God and allow our understanding of God's action in the world to evolve. What may seem to be 'true' at one point may with more knowledge and understanding be 'truer' at another.

God comes to you disguised as your life. Paula D'Arcy quoted by Richard Rohr in the Universal Christ.

So, what does my spiritualty look like today? Through my work as a psychologist and practice of yoga I have become a practitioner and teacher of mindfulness. For several years, this practice was secular, a beneficial wellbeing strategy that did good work in my mind and heart. Mindfulness taught and practised in this way is about training our attention and awareness. Cultivating mindsets such as compassion, patience, and non-judgement are also part of the practice. Mindfulness has been transformative for me, and today the practice of meditation is a form of prayer, a way of being present to what is happening now. Now when I pay attention to my breath it is with the knowledge that I am breathing in and out with the breath of the divine. Mindfulness, along with the discovery of writers such as Richard Rohr and Brian McLaren speak to my understanding of the universe; and my disillusionment and disappointment with some of the church realities of my faith.

Throughout this period of my life, I have had many conversations with my younger son about faith. He is now a minister of a regional church in Australia. This qualified electrician, with tattoos and a love of sport now also leads a church. He once said to me that I would never find a church that lived up to my expectations and there was more than an ounce of truth in this statement. However, it has helped me to bring perspective into my potential belonging to a faith community once again; and I participate in an independent, non-affiliated Church, Benedictus in an intermittent way. The minister, Sarah Bachelard is a theologian, retreat leader and a teacher in the World Community for Christian Meditation. The church has as its focus the work of silence and meditation. One of the unanticipated benefits of the Covid Pandemic, is that church has made it to the 21st century and one can now participate either face to face or on Zoom.

I must admit though, that my re-engagement with church is tenuous and cautious. I no longer wish to participate in the "big 4" mainline Christian churches, as there is so much historical baggage and even more importantly a reluctance to reform. So, I have found a space that can potentially nurture my spirit and help me make sense of the world I live in.

This is my story so far. I hope that it has given you the reader food for thought in that faith does not need to be filled with certainty to be active. If the re-examination of one's faith comes as a result of a serious health or life issue questions will be the nature of the enquiry and realignment. When it comes to recovery it is easy to underestimate the importance of meaning making; and the task of grappling with the deeper questions of life. I hope reading my story has helped you to reflect on yours.

Spirituality and human development have a reciprocal relationship, and both contribute in their own way to how we evolve as humans. If reading this leaves you puzzled or not knowing where to begin, my suggestion (taken from my reading of Brian McLaren) is to deepen your sense of self and keep on the journey to recovery. In the process, indulging your sense of curiosity and wonder may mean being surprised at what opens up for you. In the end, it is not the label that we attach to ourselves that is the most important issue, it is the commitment to live a reflective life, even a deeply contemplative one.

Postscript:

Reading these words eight years on from breast cancer are a reminder of what is deep in my heart. Today I am accompanying my parents as they reach the end of their life, and along with other significant issues, I continue to live with an uncertain faith and a hope that something is waiting for my parents when they die.

I continue to question, I continue to have doubts, but I experience such a rich sense of God's love in the very challenging day to day of my life that it no longer seems to matter. These doubts form the backdrop to my life, but the foreground is filled with beauty and colour. Little moments that have big meaning, energy despite the exhaustion and the sense that in my core, in the deepest part of me I am ok, no matter how turbulent and emotional this phase is.

I am grateful for this realisation, that my years of a doubt filled and questioning faith have prepared me for the uncertainty that comes when people you love are suffering or nearing the end of their life. I feel that I am both excelling at uncertainty in some ways and still trying to steer my way through it. What connects me to my faith now and how do I embrace a sense of God? For me little moments of wonder and curiosity, moments of feeling satisfaction and joy, laughing with my very ill mother, connecting with family and even my pet dog Holly all combine into a rich tapestry of God's enduring presence in my life. As time goes on it is not the language I have for God that helps me to understand my faith rather it is these little moments full of meaning that are the expression of what I believe.

13

BLOOM WHERE YOU ARE PLANTED

The fires swept Duffy on 18 January 2003, taking with them most of the houses on our street. Fortunately, ours was one of four to be spared. The plants on our front porch were burnt beyond recognition and our garden razed to the ground. Amazingly the pots on the porch started to regenerate within ten days of being savagely burnt. The green shoots emerged with freshness that was hard to believe given the desolation around us.

Similarly, our roses remained but as charred stumps which looked like all life had been sucked out of them and we contemplated pulling them out with the rest of the burnt debris from our garden. We decided to wait and from the flush of stumps was the most magnificent blooming we'd ever had.

My name is Margaret and when this topic was suggested for a women's breakfast talk, I thought why now Lord? What will I be confronting as I prepare for this talk? What am I about to learn from you at this time, because right now I am finding it hard to bloom where I am planted.

I have worked for thirty-eight years with deaf children and one of my primary missions was to encourage my students to reach their full potential- to be the very best they could be wherever they were and in whatever they did. To be the 'can do' kids not the 'can't do' kids. This sometimes meant wearing an FM device or cochlea implant when they didn't want to because it didn't look cool. It meant giving a talk in class just like everyone else did, even though it took great courage.

God has given each one of us uniqueness, a talent, a skill, one that is ours alone to use in honouring him. How can we be the best we can be, wherever we are and whatever we do? How can we bloom where we are planted?

Two perspectives come to mind

- Our relationship with God
- Seasons in our lives

Beginning with our relationship with God, Psalm 39 says paraphrased from The Message

God investigate our lives
Get all the facts first hand
We're an open book to you
Even from a distance you know what we are thinking
You know when we leave and when we get back
We're never out of your sight
You know everything we are going to say before we start the first sentence
We look behind us and you are there
Then up ahead you are there too
Your reassuring presence coming and going
This is much too wonderful, we can't take it all in.

What a beautiful message for us! What a comfort to take in each day with our relationship with God! Each of us was born prepacked—for a purpose. Just how well he knows us! What intimacy we can have with Him if we take all He has to offer us and embrace it with both hands. God equips us with special and unique tools to achieve His purpose and to fulfil His plan. When we find some small space to 'be still', when we find time to pray, even if it is only arrow prayers in a busy life, when we seek His will as we approach each day just knowing that the plans he has for us are good, what a difference we will see in the blooms that grow in our life to bring glory to Him.

The second perspective is seasons in our lives. Wherever you are in your faith journey may you bloom where you are planted and subsequently be remembered by those blooms. As a little girl I spent lots of time with my grandmother while my parents played sport. My Nanna was a deeply humble and spiritual woman. She left me a gift—and understanding of what it was to love God and a hunger to understand the teaching of Jesus. Her gentleness and her quiet way of walking alongside others was a great role model for me. And now as I try and understand this season of my life it is her model that comes to me as I now rise to the test God has put before me. My garden, my situation feels a bit like the desert of Isaiah's prophesy in chapter 35:1-2

The desert ....will rejoice and blossom
Like the crocus, it will burst into bloom
All will see the glory of the Lord
The splendour of our God.

When I retired, I had the expectations and dreams of volunteering in the community, doing a course at Uni, writing children's books, travelling overseas, working in my church and spending lots of time with my husband, children and grandchildren. A different season with more choices after a season of teaching in a calling from God with the deaf.

However, my son's partner had tragic mental health and drug related issues which resulted in two of our grandchildren coming under the protection of Family Services. My son was given custody of his children two boys aged six and four. This custody was awarded provided my husband and I provided the primary care, five and a half days a week, otherwise they would be in foster care.

Our choice was clearly defined so from April that year a new lifestyle for us. Not long after our other two adult children and their families moved interstate taking with them our other nine grandchildren. These two families both with a strong Christian commitment were our tower of strength and support in this new 'parenting' role. I also live with some complicated health issues so you could understand how 'blooming where you are planted' had become a bit of a challenge. To bloom-like a flower in the desert- is to allow the God within us to rise and be visible to others.

Throughout our lives we have choices, countless choices. In this season of my life I felt like some of my choices had been taken out of my hands and in preparing for this talk I have been confronted by God to look at whether I am blooming or just existing!! And to decide what to do about that!

A small flower appears in the rock crevice as I cuddle a disturbed grandson to sleep. Another appears in the desert as I wash the toilets while on preschool roster and see the smile on my grandson's face knowing that he feels just like the other kids with a mum who comes to help. A rose starts to bud as I go weekly to teach sign language songs to my older grandson's class and hopefully will come into full bloom by the end of the term when I feel more in my comfort zone. All I do for my grandchildren is done with love and joy and the blessings I received in return are a hundredfold.

I guess I have wrestled with having my choices taken away from me when I thought I had done my 'parent' season and could now move onto the 'grandparent' season. Remember the roses that emerged triumphant after the fires even though they looked like they had all the life sucked out of them. I have the hope that my 'grandparent' season will be the most glorious yet. I also guess that I know why God created women to bear children when they are young and not when they are over sixty!!

Bloom where you are planted. This is not a command for us to be perfect. Rather it is a call for us to show God's perfect love within us.

Ludwig von Beethoven was completely deaf when he composed his ninth and most famous symphony. But even Beethoven admitted to hearing God in music and God was abundantly evident in his life. Beethoven bloomed where he was planted.

Reflect on the seasons of your life! What have you done well and what have you loved to do? In the working season of my life, teaching deaf children and working with and supporting their parents was my passion and joy. When I reflect on how I bloomed during that time I am very much aware that God was there when

I look behind me. (Psalm 139) and that gave me confidence and hope to know that He was there when I looked ahead.

Ecclesiastes chapter 3 resonated with me as I look back over the seasons of my life and see the hand of God in all my blooming.

To everything there is a season, and a time to every purpose under heaven
A time to be born, a time to die, a time to plant, and a time to pluck up that which is planted.
A time to kill, and a time to heal: a time to break down,
and a time to build up:
A time to weep, and a time to laugh; a time to mourn and a time to dance.
A time to cast away stones, and a time to gather stones together; a time to embrace, and a time to refrain from embracing.
A time to get, and a time to lose; a time to keep, and a time to cast away.
A time to rend, and a time to sew; a time to keep silence, and a time to speak.
A time to love, and a time to hate; a time of war, and a time of peace.

No matter wherever we are planted, be it in a well fertilised, well-watered, sunny location or in a place where we struggle to survive in the rocky poor soil of the desert God honours our efforts to listen to Him and our efforts to enact and enhance His plan for our lives.

My husband and I escaped for some time-out together. It was a wet and wild morning as we set out from the Sundial picnic ground, a fifteen-minute drive, south of Halls Gap. Bushes of golden heath, thyme beard- heath and notched phebalium crowded along the edges of the trails. Their scents were sharp and fragrant between our fingers; their flowers and leaves gleamed in the rain. The colours were soft pinks, creams and yellows, oranges and purples, the flowers were small and delicate. Where the rocks were bare of soil, even smaller flowers had found a way to survive, and peeped out at us from mossy hangouts in the rock crevices.

What do you need in your life to help you bloom? Do you need fire, do you need smoke, a little water or a lot, a sunny spot or shade? Can you bloom when the sun shines and when it doesn't?

Are your blooms being choked out by the roots of larger plants or your other priorities? When we look back over our lives and list what we have used to bloom in other seasons, we can refresh ourselves and get the perspective God has given to us in Psalm139.

Easter tells us that we are not alone. Our calling on this earth is to bloom, to shine in the sun, to revel in the rain, to grow, to be beautiful, to dance in the sun and to bring joy. This is our invitation to walk with the living Lord. Maybe you have health problems, a child with special needs, you are caring for a spouse or parent, or your job is draining you. Remember this is where the Lord has planted you. Bloom there. Don't wait for God to change the circumstances but with his help and the help of caring Christians, bloom where you are.

Through the ages we look at women in the Bible like Sarah who gave up her homeland, Esther whose courage saved a nation, Mary Magdalene who ministered to Jesus and Phoebe and Priscilla the leaders of the early church. These are a few women empowered by God to do work outside their comfort zone for God.

You and I are called to ministry, be it in our bold and brave season, our passionate and challenging season, our "everyday small stuff" season. This is how we bloom where we are planted.

14

CONTINUING THE JOURNEY

My name is Margaret. The story I shared in Jenny's first book was the story of my life-time journey towards ordination in the Uniting Church of Australia (UCA) at the age of 50.

Now I am going to unpack part of that story - how I changed my theological thinking. What happened that made me change the way I think about God, the Bible and the Christian life.

Like many baby boomers, my Christian beliefs were formed in Sunday School. I was born into a Christian family, but my parents were not overt about it even though Mum regularly attended the local Methodist church. My faith was simple and summed up in the old hymn "Jesus loves me this I know for the Bible tells me so." I believed God sent Jesus to die for my sins and lives in heaven with God the Father. I recall giving my life to Jesus at age 10 at an Open-air Church Campaigners rally. It was implicit that when I died, I would go to heaven because I believed in Jesus. No questions. I loved the Bible stories we were taught and excelled in Sunday School exams.

Loving what I was taught in Sunday School was just part of who I was as a child. I was a bit weird I think, because I also loved school right from the start- especially reading. In High School, literature and Biology were my favourite subjects. My attention was really grabbed in the final year of high school with Biology when we were introduced to Darwin's theory of evolution. That prompted long discussions with my mother at the kitchen sink while drying dishes. I wondered how the idea of evolution and the biblical story of creation could be reconciled. At that time, I had no real answer, so I was prepared to live with Mum's compromise eg a day in God's time might be a thousand or even a million years. But questions began –

like the flood and the impossibility of having a pair of every animal on earth being saved in Noah's ark! I questioned the feasibility of the Jonah story and more.

Youth group didn't seem to be the place to ask questions so poor mum copped the next onslaught. We were studying the gospel of John and I was intrigued with the "I am" statements of Jesus. I argued with my mother that no man in his right mind would make such statements about himself. They had to be the writer's ideas or else Jesus was an egotistical madman. "Hmmm..." said mum!

Time went on and as a young woman, life began to consume me. Questions went unanswered and gradually fell silent. I completed Teacher Training and found myself far from home. I was pregnant when I married in 1969 and became the mother of a beautiful little boy Anthony, who was quickly followed by another, Mark. Not surprisingly, the marriage did not last long and I returned to my parent's home to recover, regroup and start again.

In my difficulties, whatever faith remained was no help. Instead, my conservative thinking fed my feelings of guilt arising from my apparent failures. I felt that not only had I failed my parents, but also Jesus by not keeping to the Christian standards I had been taught. My confidence was shattered. Somehow, I survived, but only just, thanks to the loving support of my parents. I went back to work and life began again.

Iain and I met in Caringbah Methodist Church which I had started attending again (it was the church of my childhood) and where we married in 1975. After the birth of our first child Sandra, my mental health crashed. I fell into a deep post-natal depression. With prayer and support, I eventually recovered and thankfully was able to continue my life. In my first talk I referred to a "born again experience" at this time, in which I felt unexpectedly but amazingly overwhelmed by the presence of God, loving and forgiving me.

After that, my faith grew stronger. The Bible became important to me again and a source of great comfort, especially the Psalms. The questions were safely tucked away and I was content with my renewed faith. Life was good.

That state of affairs continued as we relocated to Canberra in 1980 with Iain's job just a year after the birth of our fourth child, David. The move had meant leaving behind not only family, but a very close friend, Ngaire whose friendship would continue through the years despite the physical distance between us. Meeting while I was recovering from Post Natal Depression, she was a gift from God.

We settled into life in Canberra and at first attended North Belconnen Uniting Church. After about 5 years we left for various reasons and linked up with the local Baptist Church. From here I was to begin a new journey. It was 1986, I think. The pastor preached a sermon about raising children which seemed to be directed towards Iain and me. At the time we were experiencing difficulties with our adolescent boys. The theme was the Proverbs text "spare the rod and spoil the child!" Perhaps I was oversensitive because I reacted with anger and felt betrayed after having sort his help. Where was love and mercy for the parents let alone the children??!

I was still a literal believer in the Bible but now the contradiction between a God of Grace and a God who was vengeful and advocated violence as a means of correction was "in my face" so to speak. Teaching that flew in the face of my educational understandings, the way my parents loved me unconditionally in my time of need just as we too were wanting to love our wayward boys and plain common sense.

About that time Ngaire gave me a set of tapes. They were recordings of the late Episcopal Bishop, Rev John Spong introducing his first book, "Rescuing the Bible from Fundamentalism." Writing in the 1980's he was trying to change mainstream Christianity's attitude to the Bible particularly in regard to the understanding of sexuality.

As I listened, I felt a seismic shift in my mind and soon I found myself in a scary place. No longer secure and safe in my faith cocoon, I was being challenged to systematically rethink my Christian beliefs. All the questions that had been simmering on the back burner of my life, now came to the boil.

Both Ngaire and I read all Spong's books. We began exploring our understanding of God, the Bible and the Christian faith. When we visited each other or went on family camping holidays, we always included long walks together to talk theology. What is the Bible? What is difference between God and the Bible? What can we know about God? Who is Jesus? What is the Cross about? What is salvation? What does the church have to do with Jesus and more?

The realisation that the Bible had been used to justify such things as the Crusades, burning witches or Catholics or protestants at the stake, that slavery, apartheid, denigration of first nation peoples, the sexual abuse of children, the subjugation of women and white, male heterosexual supremacy appalled me. How could this be called the Word of God? How could this book be authoritative? Why had I been shielded from such knowledge?

I thank God that I did not lose my faith completely. Many do when this realisation dawns on them. Instead, it became an exciting, intense time as I used my common sense, my life experiences, my education and my love of God to explore and question what I had taken for granted for so long. My faith grew and deepened.

Iain and I relocated to Chisholm from Kaleen in 1988. Early in 1990 we found ourselves in TUC when Rev Joyce Shietel and Rev Tony Hooper were the ministers. One of my newly found ways of understanding Scripture was standing right before my eyes. An ordained female minister with a dynamic ministry! Taking to heart a text from Isaiah, I continued my quest for understanding. Isaiah 43:19-21 (NRSV) I am about to do a new thing; now it springs forth, do you not perceive it? I will make a way in the wilderness and rivers in the desert. The wild animals will honour me, the jackals and the ostriches; for I give water in the wilderness, rivers in the desert, to give drink to my chosen people, the people whom I formed for myself so that they might declare my praise.

Ngaire had begun a Degree in Theology a couple years before this and now I began biblical studies at St Mark's here in Canberra and the rest is history... so they say. It is a great privilege to be a member of the UCA for the Basis of Union encourages each of us to have faith with understanding.

Since my ordination twenty four years ago, (December 2001,) the practice of ministry has continued to inform and shape me. Yes, old dogs can learn new tricks! My language for God has changed from being exclusively male to reflect God who is neither male nor female. Choosing hymns has become interesting since many hymns that were once among my favourites, espouse a theology with which is no longer mine or use language that is no longer appropriate in an inclusive community. I struggle saying the creeds and no longer hold as literally true many other aspects of our faith such as the birth stories of Jesus. However, I no longer have any difficulty reading the faith stories of Creation and understanding the theory of evolution. I could say much more but perhaps that is for another time.

In my retirement, I am still learning new skills, gaining new knowledge, continuing to question and yes, wrestle with doubt. The journey goes on and is still shared with my friend Ngaire who now lives in her homeland Aotearoa New Zealand where she is a lay preacher and leader in her local Methodist church. When we can visit each other, long walks and theological discussions still happen – including on Zoom. Many other old and new friends, as well as colleagues, support and encourage me, many of whom are members of TUC, not the least of which is my patient (but sometimes not so patient) husband Iain.

No two journeys are ever the same. No one way is better than any other. Wherever you are in your faith journey, whether you are travelling in certainty or worry that you have lost your way or are somewhere in between, be assured you are loved and cherished by our God – whose wisdom is beyond our knowing yet who is as close as your next breath. May the One who is Life and Love remain with us as we continue together as pilgrims on the road.

15

A JOURNEY OF SELF DISCOVERY

am I a phony?

My name is Marjorie and I think my faith journey began on a Sunday afternoon in Sydney where for a few weeks I had been going along to an outdoor Sunday School run by the Open Air Campaigners in a suburban park. I was 11 years old, and enjoyed sitting on the grass singing the songs and listening to the stories, and when eventually I was asked by one of the workers if I would like to invite Jesus to come and live in my heart, I said yes, I would like to do that, and I prayed that little prayer. I remember singing, "Into my heart, come into my heart Lord Jesus. Come in today, come in to stay, come into my heart, Lord Jesus".

It was many years however before I understood the significance of that 'ask', but a year or so later I linked up with the North Bondi Methodist Church, and this did its best to nurture and grow me. Sadly, my parents who were not Christians, were unable to give me any positive teaching or support, in fact my father, for reasons I never fully understood, was opposed to any form of Christianity. Most helpful though as I grew older was the Christian group I joined and belonged to for 5 years at Sydney University, the Evangelical Union, which provided fun, fellowship and friendship, social support and consistent Christian teaching. By the end of my university days, when I was starting to look for a social work position and preparing to marry Jim, I think I understood fairly clearly who Jesus was and why I wanted to have an ongoing relationship with him. And I was very happy about this.

However, out in the real world as I came to know more about the church generally, I began to realise I had absorbed a very conservative evangelical understanding of the faith, which at the time made complete sense to me, even though it did not relate to any personal issues, or as far as I could see, to the needs of society. But in those days, I didn't think I had any personal problems, and I wasn't much bothered by society's problems either. But as time passed and I continued to mature, life itself began to confront me with many difficult situations which I found difficult to reconcile with that earlier teaching.

By then I had married, worked for 4 years as a social worker in the Dept of the Interior which ran Canberra in those days, gone overseas with my modern languages' teacher husband, had my first child in England, travelled all around the UK, lived for a year in Germany, finally returning to Australia in 1963. By 1969 we were back in Canberra. This was because Jim, who was also trying to live out God's call on his life, believed that as he prayed, God opened doors and led him graciously through. In this instance the Commonwealth Office of Education where he was working at the time, had been compulsorily transferred to Canberra. We were both pleased to be back, living in Cook, attending O'Connor Methodist Church, and caring now for 4 children. By then I had been 18 years out of the workforce and was beginning to contemplate a return to part-time work. I was still living out of my conservative theology but no longer happy in it. But major changes were ahead and I would like to share with you three areas of spirituality and faith where I have come to understand things differently. The first concerned my relationship with God the father, the second, the way I related to others, and the third, the way I lived in the wider world.

First, my relationship with God. Although I knew Jesus was very much part of my life, I felt disconnected from God the father, for in my evangelical theology he was the one who judged and condemned. I took my place in the universal depravity of the human race very seriously and did not believe that God could really love me. I know now that this derived partly from my childhood, as my parents had not been able to foster any sense of self-worth inside me even though I knew they loved me, but it was not customary then to praise or affirm the positives in your children in case you gave them a 'swelled head', and also they were not very good at expressing their feelings. I was probably predisposed to take on board God's judgement of my sinful human nature. After all, "all my righteousness was as filthy rags in his sight", was it not?

While I was feeling very miserable about all this two, things began to happen more or less simultaneously. First, the church went into charismatic renewal (I say we experienced a baptism of love) and second, I was accepted into a training program run by the Canberra Marriage Guidance Council. I had applied for this because I knew I would need some kind of refresher course if I were to seek a social work position, and this was the nearest thing available. I was put into a small group to test my readiness for training. I didn't know at the time that it was an Encounter Group.

I joined the group with a miniscule amount of self-understanding but one thing I was aware of in my heart of hearts, was that I had become somewhat of a chameleon. Chameleons are a kind of lizard able to change their colour in order to blend in with their environment. I seemed to have the ability to suss out what people liked or valued, and in order to be accepted by them, would then do my best to be like them, changing colour metaphorically speaking, to fit in. I was desperate for approval but was surrendering my real self (not that I knew what that was) to get people to like me. But gradually, as I began to open myself up to the Holy Spirit in a new way, I was given a fresh understanding of God's love, and a deep process of healing began inside me, based on the fact that God knew all about me and loved me anyway. (That is not saying by the way that there was no room for improvement). Looking back now I think I had failed to understand the significance of being made in the image of God, that there was, as the Quakers have always said 'that of God in every human being', an element of goodness and a capacity to love in all of us, including me, despite the capacity we also have to choose to withhold love, and do evil.

And the Marriage Guidance encounter group? God used it to bring me to my senses. When I started I was still well into my chameleon persona, playing a sympathetic role to the other members who were being much more open and honest, variously falling apart and being put together again by the combined positivity of the group. I had told my husband early on that there was one person in the group for whom I felt particularly sorry. Imagine my surprise when on the last night this young woman confronted me by saying, "You know Marjorie, I feel sorrier for you than for anyone else in this group, because ......you're a phony". She was absolutely right, but after recovering from the shock I replied to her from an inner strength and authenticity I didn't know I had. I went home that night and said to my husband, "I feel as if I have been born again". And in one sense I had. The chameleon was thanked and given its marching orders while I embarked on a journey of self discovery and acceptance and was never quite the same again.

My experience is supported by a book *Emotionally Healthy Spirituality,* written by a pastor who successfully ran a large church until the day his wife said to him, "I'm leaving your church. You are one thing on the outside and another on the inside". Across the front of this book these words are written horizontally: It is impossible to be spiritually mature while remaining emotionally immature. A challenging statement, emphasising the need to become more self-aware, so that we can bring our various hang-ups to God for healing. Very few of us if any, had a perfect childhood, mainly because we were raised by human beings. But the more we can truly accept ourselves as completely loved by God and companioned by Jesus, the more we can actually look at feelings or memories which may have been outside our conscious awareness for years, but which nevertheless impinged on all our relationships and behaviours, and the more God can help us grow emotionally and spiritually. We need not be overwhelmed by this process, because God is kind and loving, and the Holy Spirit has many, many ways of helping us along this journey of becoming more whole, and more holy. The Biblical word for this is sanctification.

At this point life became much happier for me. I got my part-time job, ironically as a mental health social worker, and loved it, learnt a lot through professional development programs particularly in the area of Loss and Grief. A newfound faith – Jim and I both working on our emotional/spiritual maturity, part of a supportive home group, and Jim privileged to be working in the Community Relations Commission under Al Grassby. We seemed very settled, facing challenging questions together.

The second area in my life which underwent revision was how I related to others. Was my behaviour consistent with Jesus' words? Did I love my neighbour as much as myself? How do I react when people hurt me? Do I repay evil with evil? What about people who are different? Jesus had plenty to say about such matters. Exactly how do I act justly, love mercy and walk humbly with my Lord? Am I willing to live simply so that others may simply live? I guess we each answer these questions as God leads us, respecting one another's views.

And then came the bad news, Malcolm Fraser abolished the Community Relations Commission in 1983 and my husband was out of a job! Shock and horror! However, amazingly another door opened right out of the blue! The Victorian Council of Churches wanted a project officer to promote multicultural awareness amongst Melbourne theological colleges and churches. Jim was delighted to be offered that position, so a big move happened in March 1984 as we set off with two boys, a dog and a cat for Melbourne. The project was to be funded for 18 months, so expecting to return when it was completed, we did not sell our house in Canberra. But would you believe that Jim's belief in opening doors was confirmed again when at the end of the project, the then Archbishop of Melbourne David Penman invited him to consider ordination as an Anglican priest. He was 55 years old. This was a much more challenging open door! And I wasn't sure that I could become a vicar's wife! But after a great deal of praying, soul-searching and procrastinating, and thanks to what God had done and was continuing to do in my life, I finally felt brave enough to walk through that door with him. We remained in Melbourne mostly in parish ministry, for the next 36 years.

I loved the first parish Jim was appointed to, St Mary Magdalene's in the suburb of Dallas, and threw myself fully into supporting his ministry, resigning from my job and enrolling to do a diploma course in Community Development. Dallas had the lowest socio-economic indicators in the whole of Melbourne and most Melburnians had never heard of it. There were 14 people present at our first service. The challenge was to accept, love and encourage, to come alongside and visit, and keep on visiting. To offer the few crumbs we had in our hands as wounded healers ourselves, to people even more vulnerable. I was very sad when the time came to leave seven years later as many beautiful things had happened, one of them the beautiful girls' liturgical dance group, and another the home group we set up for the very dysfunctional family which could not cope with an Anglican church service. I received a hundredfold more love and blessing than I ever gave in that parish.

Then came St Michael's, where a young vibrant Cantonese-speaking congregation was being grafted onto an elderly Anglo one. We loved it there too, Jim was the associate minister and I was licensed by the Archbishop as an authorised lay minister, to do pastoral care with the English speakers. From there we went three times to China, giving English conversation practice to students and teachers at one of the 19 universities in the huge inland city of Chongqing. Once again we received far more than we gave.

Then finally retirement, parishioners now at our local Anglican parish, which was about to embark on a Journey of Reconciliation with the local Wurundjeri people. I was privileged to write the final report of that journey. And then farewell to Melbourne and hello again to Canberra, with the joy and privilege of being part of Tuggeranong Uniting Church. You have made me so very welcome and I thank you from the bottom of my heart. I'm waiting now for my Final Door to open, which opened for Jim on 27 December 2022. After 66 years of marriage, I still miss him very much.

But what about my third spiritual awakening? The way I lived in God's beautiful creation. In this area I have been greatly helped by some early Celtic Christian beliefs, which emphasise the sacredness of all creation, and see the physical world as a holy mystery to be respected, cared for and lived within. For them there was no arbitrary divide between sacred and secular, God is in everything, from the most majestic mountain to the tiniest flower bud. They also believed that if God is good, there is something of that goodness in every human person, and that the only way to overcome the darkness in their hearts which was there as well as the good, was to pursue what they understood as the light, which was the life of Christ. Their spiritual goal is to be on a life-long journey into Christ-likeness.

I also hold in high regard the present Iona Community in Scotland, seen both as the cradle of Christianity in Scotland and the focus of the modern interest in Celtic spirituality. This community is known for its joyful and celebratory music, its creative liturgies and life-embracing prayers. In addition, it sees itself as a radical movement committed to living out the Christian faith in the areas of human rights, environmental stewardship, non-violence, healing and reconciliation. It is concerned for all who are oppressed and works cooperatively with anyone who shares these commitments. This is so different from my earlier understanding of the faith. Some years ago, Jim and I joined the Wellspring Community, Iona's daughter organisation in Australia. Wellspring's motto is "where spirituality and justice meet", hence an emphasis on peace and biblical justice, the health of our planet, and a desire for true reconciliation with Australia's first peoples.

So where am I today? Made in the image of God, and I hope, growing into the likeness of Christ. Much more in touch with the God whom Jesus described when he told the Pharisees the story of the father and the two sons. Their God was a book-keeping, rule- making God who could not tolerate the 'sinners' Jesus was associating with; they deserved judgement and ostracism, not friendship, affirmation or healing. But Jesus pictured an entirely different God, one who embraced failures, who ran to welcome the son returning home – the son who had virtually wished his father dead – and didn't even allow him to finish his penitential speech before hugging him and ordering the celebration. Jesus' God is the father who also sought out his older son, begging him to come to the party too. I would like to be one of that group of Christians who are living with images of God which affirm and build up, bring life and engender hope, also seeing women as sacred, and as holy as men.

I want to become more like that man from Galilee, who befriended outcasts, loved his friends, elevated women, practised and taught forgiveness, and who had compassion on all who were suffering. Yes, I have thrown out a lot of bathwater over the years but I have never walked away from Jesus.

16

CODDIWOMPLING INTO MINISTRY

My name is Sharon and *Coddiwomple* is a word that was gifted to me early on in my formation for ministry. My understanding of its definition is to "confidently stride out towards some unknown destination." Here's my story of coddiwompling into ministry.

I was born into a loving Christian family who was seriously involved in the Anglican Church. As the youngest of three girls Church was a way of life, I loved Sunday School, tolerated the church clothes that my mother sewed for me, and miracles happened. One miracle I remember is praying earnestly to find a precious silver bangle that I had lost, getting the impression that I should lift up the rug – and there it was! I was deeply relieved and grateful.

My mother became very ill. We shifted to our Kiwi capital,Wellington, to meet her medical needs for her cancer, but there were no miracles there and we lost her. I was 10 years old.

We were all still very involved in church and youth group. I coordinated the Sunday School and became an Inter School Christian Fellowship leader - after following a chocolate cake to an ISCF meeting - and "became" a Christian at a Youth For Christ rally. Christian camps were THE BEST. I always thought that this would be as the Vicar's wife – choir, flowers, cooking roast dinners on Sundays after church for all the waifs and strays. Women weren't ordained in those days!

At Victoria University of Wellington, I attended Presbyterian, Methodist, Anglican, Baptist and Catholic churches with my friends, but it wasn't till I started teachers' training in Christchurch that I renewed my involvement of being an active member of the

Anglican Church at St James's, Riccarton.

Back in Wellington, I had made an intellectual reaffirmation of my faith for prayer and bible study but – the day before I started teaching, I experienced a charismatic re-formation. I remember walking into my first full staff meeting and someone asked loudly, "My God, does it always smile like that?" I was glowing and excited to be starting my first ever teaching post at Wellington East Girls' College. I was again leading the ISCF group and a had full-on involvement with Anglican Renewal and many conferences and camps ensued. A few years later I later stepped into more University studies - the eternal student that I am - while taking up the role of the Anglican Lay Chaplain at Victoria University of Wellington. This was testing the waters of ministry under the Order of St Stephen.

And then I met the man I married – Kerry. He lived in Christchurch, so I became the Lay Chaplain at Christchurch Teachers' College and Christchurch Polytech (TAFE) and I shifted in across the road from him, seeing he unknowingly adopted all my old community of Christchurch friends.

While painting a fence (with sump oil of course!) I had a sense of calling and agreed that if I was called to ministry that I would say yes. To quote Monty Python, "Suddenly, nothing happened."

We moved to Edinburgh, Scotland – as one does – following the man's career. Two children arrived and we shifted to Melbourne, from the Anglican church to Uniting. I returned to teaching full time but - following my son's diagnosis of Autism Spectrum Disorder - I returned to study – this time Psychology! Highly pertinent to my circumstances.

Canberra called. We moved. I became a Pastoral Care Assistant at Mirinjani Village. Leading worship, pastoral visiting, memorial services and funerals as requested. I became the Children's Church Administrator at Wesley in Forrest and then completed the Sacraments Course. My boss – the Chaplain – did the course with me and was required to begin theological study to train as a Pastor and my heart jumped – "Me Too!" I quietly set this aside awaiting confirmation that this was God calling, and not just me.

At Wesley I often led the liturgy when my husband preached. About a year after the sacraments course, he had spent hours preparing a sermon. I had spent less than an hour preparing the liturgy. They were both good, but more people praised the liturgy more than the sermon. Kerry was less than impressed but he relayed to me a comment that his valued mentor and friend made along the lines of "Ah, but we all know that Sharon is destined for ministry."

Suddenly there was a burst of joy in my heart and then complete and utter peace. A peace that has always guided me in major life choices, so I was convinced that I should follow this path. A path of obedience.

What confirmed this was when I was preparing a Children's Church lesson and a verse jumped out at me. "What you began a year ago, now bring to completion." (2 Corinthians 8:7-15) O my goodness. I had such a conviction that I was being called that I told my husband, the Chaplain leading the team I was on at Mirinjani Village and all the ministers at Wesley - David Thiem, Alastair Christie and Ockert Meyer.

I rang the Uniting Church of Australia (UCA) head office and was informed that I would have to shift to Sydney! Like that could happen with two kids on the Autism Spectrum and my professor husband at ANU!!!

I was accepted onto the Regional Ministry Formation Program based in Canberra but I had no actual intention of being ordained. I applied to be a Minister of Deacon. God said No – you will be Minister of the Word. Okay!

Study followed. Lots of study. I loved it. It was an escape from parenting. It was an escape from my grief after Kerry died. It was obedience to a call with no clear end in sight. I completed a Grad Dip in Theology and then a Masters, MA (Theol.)

Covid had hit and church with my son was not a possibility as he had become an angry young man and my eldest chose not to come to church. On holidays down the coast, I snuck off to church while my teenage kids were sleeping. I looked at people up the front being ministers and I finally agreed. Okay God – you want me to be up the front there? I guess so.

My son Nick moved out of home enabling me to complete my ministry formation here at Tuggeranong Uniting Church – and here I am – now ordained. It is still a surprise. And I am still confidently striding out towards some unknown destination of ministry with the wonderful people here at Tuggeranong Uniting.

17

THE BEAUTY OF LOOKING BACK

My name is Sue and I share with you my story with excitement and humility because God has given me this life and He's given me Alison as my daughter and that as you will see is a tremendous blessing.

My story is not an extraordinary story but an ordinary story of everyday faith and life. I love stories and perhaps that's why I trained as a Teacher Librarian. I particularly love how God uses our stories to encourage others and to help us persevere. I hope you will see as we travel through my story that God at work in the ordinary. Stories involve a journey and my story is no different. Remembering is good for us. It reminds us of God's faithfulness and what he has done for us. The Israelites remembered throughout the Old Testament. They remembered crossing the Red Sea, the Passover, entering the promised land and I'm sure you can think of other examples. They remembered God's faithfulness, his love, his mercy, his compassion and the New Testament Jesus says "do this in remembrance of me" as he demonstrated to the disciples the Lord's Supper. Jesus wants us to remember His death and resurrection and what that achieved for us and who we now are in Him.

Lamentations 3:22-23 is pertinent to my story

Because of the Lord's great love we are not consumed, for his compassions never fail. They are new every morning, great is your faithfulness.

Knowing that God's faithfulness and His mercies are new every morning is what has and continues to hold me in my story. My family consists of myself and John, Luke our eldest, Alison and Andrew the youngest and their partners. Our new addition to our family, beautiful Poppy – a groodle puppy.

This part of my story begins in 1984 when our second child was born, a girl, Alison. A beautiful healthy baby girl, until we began to notice that she was not developing as well as we thought she should. She was slow with her milestones – sitting, crawling, walking and she had low muscle tone. We began the road of investigating that with a paediatrician and later with educational testing to explore exactly what was going on. What came out of that did not seem to be much of a blessing to me at the time, as we were quickly on a treadmill of appointments for physiotherapy, occupational therapy, speech therapy, an intervention playgroup, and a home program. I had two little boys by that stage too and preschool to fit in.

I was largely overwhelmed and if it wasn't for the support of our church family being like Jesus to me in action. I never would have coped. I felt a failure as a mother because I couldn't do it all myself – other mothers did – so why not me! I grieved seeing my daughter not being able to keep up with her peers both physically and intellectually and I grieved through her unreasonable behaviour should the routines have to change. Alison was eventually diagnosed with an intellectual delay and later Autism Spectrum Disorder.

The journey had begun and I had no idea how God was going to use that story to grow me, to enlarge my heart with love for others and show me just how great his faithfulness is. But this is how God works through the ordinary. He puts people and events in our daily lives to help us and teach us.

Romans 8:28 *All things work together for good for those who love God and are called according to His purposes*, has stayed with me throughout this story – a verse I had read and heard many times but that I now had to cling to and still do. You will see it again and again in my story.

I wanted a mainstream education for Alison. In fact, I wanted more than that, I wanted a Christian education for her. It was what we had chosen for our other children and what we wanted for Alison too as one of our family. But there were barriers. The Christian school suggested they did not have the resources they needed to support Alison and so, I am embarrassed to say, it was with some reluctance that I went to the public system. Even then, I was stubbornly determined and said that if she was going to a Junior Assessment Class, she was going to the one I picked! Not long after I began a Graduate Diploma in Special Education because I wanted to be an authority and not just a parent. I had been recommended Taylor Primary School by a couple of different sources so I thought, and convinced my husband that, this was God's leading.

We sought to buy a house in the catchment area for that school, and we were already attending church nearby anyway. How we bought that house was amazing as I look back because we couldn't find what we wanted. My parents suggested that we put an ad in the paper. House wanted! Who does that! I don't think we really thought we'd achieve anything, but God had other ideas. A lady was reading the paper that Saturday. She was a widow and it had been suggested to her that she move to Tasmania closer to her son as her daughter with Down's Syndrome had been staying with her brother. We bought her house and just a walk to Taylor Primary School.

Alison stayed at Taylor until the end of year 5 beginning of year 6. I started knocking on the door of the Christian school again saying that they had to decide now as we had to make decisions for High School. I was a parent at the school.

They agreed to investigate and educate the staff and students. A small committee of which I was a part began to do that. We ran workshops with teachers and student leadership, we liaised with the Canberra University and organised for the Special Education professor to come and speak to staff. We made our case to the School Council who agreed to employ a special educator in the Year that Alison entered Year 7.

Once more the body of believers supported Alison with people from our church coming into the school to volunteer as teacher's aides. We were even privileged to have the principal's wife support her in class. I have never forgotten what people gave up to help us be trail blazers. The intake of children with special needs grew and has grown over the years. I have no idea how we had the foresight we did, and I can only put that down to God leading and enabling of us.

Long before school-based apprenticeships were available we explored this for our daughter, being convinced that it would be her reliability as a worker rather than her academic results that would get her work. From Year 7 she had half a day a week at various placements. Alison got a job after school and worked for seven years in a well-known fast-food restaurant. Then followed a couple more jobs at a childcare centre and a costume shop before getting the job she has now at an event venue. Alison has been with her current employer now for ten years and was recently recognised for her years of service. It was a proud mum and dad moment, and I think she is proud of her own achievement too. I can't sing the praises of this employer and its employees more highly. They are truly inclusive, and I can tell by her interactions with them that they respect and like her for who she is. God has provided and placed her exactly where she needs to be.

Not in my wildest imaginings could I have foreseen how God was going to lead us to moving Alison from our family home into her own home, but God had this in hand well in advance. We had been encouraged to look at moving Alison out of the family home. We had thought that if she was to move out it would be to somewhere we owned and not to a group home as we wanted her to be somewhere that had the same values as us and the values we had encouraged her to have for herself. How it came about however is in my mind nothing short of a miracle.

My husband had received a redundancy package and with that came financial advice which we duly followed and kept following until the time John was 54 when he was advised to salary sacrifice all of his pay that year because he, no one else and purely because of the redundancy, could get a certain amount of money out of his super fund at 55. We duly did as we were told and when the time arrived got the money out and paid off the remainder of our own home mortgage. Now we thought we are in a position to save for a deposit for something for Alison.

That was not to happen. I was at church for a meeting one day and I went out to the foyer to talk to my son on the phone. As I chatted, I looked on the notice board – I never looked on the notice board but there on the board was an advertisement for a townhouse. We had one criteria next to money – one bus and then looking into Bonython there was one bus to Tuggeranong and one bus to Woden. We went and had a look, talked to the bank and borrowed the whole amount. Then something else amazing happened. The school counsellor at the school I was working at asked if she could house share with Alison. She needed to move before we settled and so we came to arrangement with the seller whom we both knew. He was a teacher at the school. We couldn't have chosen a better person to live with Alison - kind, caring, supportive, experienced in ASD and ID and she had a house full of furniture! After we settled, we moved Alison in one night at a time until she was there permanently. Eventually Jenny, her housemate moved out to her own place. We tried a couple of other arrangements which weren't that successful, so I asked Alison is she wanted to live by herself and she agreed. That is over 10 years ago now and with the support of NDIS, she lives there successfully and with quite a degree of independence.

NDIS has been and continues to be a game changer for us. We have fabulous support workers and friends and she has fabulous friends at church who all add to her life. One of our support workers is a Christian and another lady who does some reading and writing skills with her is a Christian. She often reads the Bible with Alison as part of the tutoring. Alison likes to make cards for people and all through COVID she made cards for people in other places who were in lockdown. She continues to make cards. She and Anneke often make and write cards as part of their session. They are cards that encourage others. The cards have become Alison's ministry to others. Alison also attends the women's bible study at church and is well loved. She goes to a group fortnightly called Friends of Jesus that is specifically for adults with a disability that runs at the church. I think Alison has a good life and I think if you asked her she would agree – and I'm thankful for that as we need to set her up for a time in the future when we won't be able to care for her.

I started with these verses, Lamentations 3:22-23 and Romans 8:28

Because of the Lord's great love we are not consumed, for his compassions never fail. They are new every morning great is your faithfulness.

All things work together for good for those who love God and are called according to His purposes. – not just some things but ALL things.

I'd hate to leave the impression that all things have been wonderful and rosy. There have been trials – stress on our family, tantrums, anxiety, unwise decisions with unwanted consequences, fear, grief - but God works them all together for good and for his glory.

Knowing God's goodness and mercy and His faithfulness and looking back at how He has sustained us over the past almost 40 years is an amazing blessing. It helps us move forward to the next stage and reminds me when I am tempted to worry that God hasn't let us down yet and will continue to be faithful.

Sometimes I have even looked at this story and I have to pinch myself because it makes me wonder - Is this MY life! God does immeasurably more than I could ever hope or expect. His ways are not my ways or His timing, my timing but He is in control – ALWAYS.

God led me into areas I would never have imagined I would go. I worked in special needs education for about 20 years, I started the Friends of Jesus group, I have spoken to parents, I have helped others navigate NDIS and more. I am not a natural born leader, but God has placed me in situations where I have had to step outside of the boat so to speak, be outside of my comfort zone and trust Him to help me.

I want to leave you with another verse that means more and more to me as life passes.

Mark 8:36 *What good is it for a man if he gains the whole world yet forfeits their soul.*

I thought Alison was missing out. I thought we were missing out, but she has achieved and is achieving much and just maybe because there is a part of her that still thinks like a child, it's easier for her to come to Jesus than for all of us.

Jesus says Let the little children come to me ... For the kingdom of God belongs to them. And It is easier for a camel to go through the eye of a needle than it is for a rich person to enter the Kingdom of God.

That's the thing that we want for ourselves our family and our friends those we come in contact with – to know Christ and to be in his kingdom above all else and Alison knows this, whilst at this stage of their lives, her brothers have walked away from faith.

My encouragement to you from my story.

Look back:

1 Remember God's faithfulness to you.

2 Look back and remember that God was in control then and He still is.

3 Remember that God knows the bigger plan. *For my thoughts are not your thoughts, neither are your ways my ways declares the Lord. As the heavens are higher than the earth, so are my ways higher than your ways and my thoughts than your thoughts.* (Is 55:8-9)

Look forward, being confident that *He who began a good work in you will carry it on to completion until the day of Christ Jesus.* (Phil 1:8)

Live now in the present, trusting in

1 God's faithfulness,

2 His compassion

3 His mercies knowing that they are new every morning and

> knowing that whatever the circumstances that NOTHING - *not death nor life, neither angels or demons, neither the present or the future, nor any powers, neither height nor depth nor anything in all creation, will be able to separate us from the love of God that is in Christ Jesus.* (Romans 8:38-39)

This is what helps me to stand firm in the faith and helps me to grow more like Jesus. Thank you for the opportunity to encourage you because the Lord has done good to me and I do want to give Him the praise and glory for His goodness and grace. Totally undeserved and yet given anyway.

Psalm 13: 5-6 *But I trust in your unfailing love, my heart rejoices in your salvation. I will sing to the Lord, for He has done good to me.*

Thanks be to God!

18

THE BOOKMARK

For I know the plans I have for you declares the Lord, plans to prosper you and not to harm you, plans to give you hope and a future.
Jeremiah 29:11.

My name is Sue and I was fortunate to grow up in a loving Christian home with my mother and father having met each other at church youth group and continuing to attend church wherever they lived.

As the oldest of three children, I have vague memories of living in Melbourne (twice) and Suva in Fiji, but it is living in the southern suburbs of Sydney where I lived for most of my childhood that I can most clearly remember. We lived at Woronora and our family attended an Anglican Church a few suburbs away. My parents had, as they always did no matter where we lived, sought out the church that they thought was most welcoming and aligned with their beliefs.

My childhood was a happy one. My father worked as a chemical engineer travelling quite a bit, while my mother worked in our home raising children and looking after us all.

I was a quiet and shy child and my parents' expectations that we attend the church youth groups after we were too old for Sunday School, was a challenging one for me. It was fine in theory having Christian friends and getting to know the Lord more as a group together, but the reality was that I didn't really feel like I fitted in. The others all knew each other from school and living nearby the church. No matter how hard I tried it was always difficult and not a very comfortable place to be. At that time, I don't think I really felt I knew God well enough to trust in Him to find a way forward for me in that situation.

Nevertheless, I really enjoyed being a Sunday School teacher and working with the children. I'd had some really inspirational and faithful Sunday School teachers when I was smaller, and I was keen to explore God's Word with the younger children. They really didn't care what school I went to.

After I finished university, I moved to Canberra for work. Around the time of my last year of university the biggest employer of agricultural science graduates, the NSW government, ceased employing graduates as agricultural extension officers. So I, and most of my fellow students, needed to look further afield for work. My job in Canberra involved educating students about a parasite affecting both animals and humans. I think it was likely that one of the reasons I got that job was because of my Sunday School teaching experience.

I met my husband through work and we began our life together in Canberra. We got married at Tuggeranong Uniting Church but given various other factors we weren't regular church goers.

Time moved on and we had a much -loved child to add to our family of my husband's two children. I continued to work, travel for work and do the best I could. Things were not always easy but on reflection I can say that God was always with me and provided great comfort and peace whenever I asked and needed it. Before I knew it one day in early 2016 (our daughter had finished year 12 the previous year) and after returning home from a family day trip to the coast, my husband unexpectedly died.

After some upheaval and wondering what to do now, I visited Tuggeranong Uniting Church (TUC) to see the kind of church where the very accommodating and friendly minister who had conducted my husband's funeral worked. From the first moment I walked into TUC for that Sunday service I felt at home, not judged just accepted and welcomed. It was the first time I had felt like that in a church, with no need to prove myself I could just be me.

At some point in my first few weeks at TUC I was handed the

welcome pack and a bookmark with the words *For I know the plans I have for you declares the Lord, plans to prosper you and not to harm you, plans to give you hope and a future'.* Jeremiah 29:11. What a support and comfort it was that God and this church wanted me and although my life had changed God had plans for me. I wasn't sure what plans there were for me at that stage, so I was very pleased that God did.

I really feel that God had plans for me. I have made many wonderful friends at my church and have been privileged to be part of a welcoming and accepting faith community where I have been able to grow in my love for and relationship with God. I really enjoy being part of TUC and being able to help out with some small parts of the functioning of the church such as welcoming people before the service (what a joy it is to be able to say hello to everyone who is coming to the service, not only the few people one has the opportunity to talk with after the service), pressing the PowerPoint buttons, helping out with morning tea, church council and other contributions as they come up.

One of my lovely friends from TUC suggested that I attend Bible Study Fellowship (BSF) with her. I really had no idea what this was, but it was a wonderful eye opener for me, a really in-depth study of God's Word in many layers. This was just what the newly returned to God and church me needed. It also seemed like God had plans for me there too, becoming part of the leadership group at BSF – a wonderful group of ladies whose faith reminds and encourages me again and again to grow closer and more faithful to God. God had given me the practical opportunity to contribute and serve Him by having less family obligations and being able to attend both the weekly Bible study and also the weekly leadership meetings. I was to learn that this is often a difficult ask for potential BSF leaders, with balancing the needs of their families.

Work has also been another blessing for me and a place where I can now fully contribute and God has increased my skills and opportunities there too. As I now look towards retirement from work and likely moving closer to my family, I wonder what other plans God has for me that include Him. I hope there are many.

The Lord Himself goes before you and will be with you; He will never leave you or forsake you. Do not be afraid; do not be discouraged. Deuteronomy 31:8

19

SOMETHING BEAUTIFUL, SOMETHING GOOD

Something Beautiful, Something good
All my confusion He understood.
All I had to offer Him was brokenness and strife.
But He made something beautiful of my life.

Some of you will remember this chorus and it is if you like my theme song. This is my story of how it became just that.

My name is Sue. I grew up in Sydney and like nearly all Church of England children of nominal Christian homes I went to Sunday School, was christened and confirmed but in all honesty, it meant very little. Sunday School taught me the stories of Jesus and for that I am thankful to all those faithful Sunday School teachers.

My father was a solicitor and when I was eleven, I said to Dad, "I want to be a solicitor." Dad's comment at the time was "I don't believe in women solicitors." But being very much my father's daughter, I persevered and in 1965 joined my father's firm as an articled law clerk. This was like an apprenticeship to a master solicitor. We worked full time, studied and sat our exams in our own time. We had no lectures, no notes. It was hard work. We law clerks had to work together. In the 1960s, law was a male dominated profession, female numbers were negligible. And to say we were treated poorly is to understate it. So, I decided that in order to survive in this world, I had to keep up with the boys. This involved lots of drinking and partying. I was a wild child, coming home at all hours and causing my parents lots of grief. It was also in the sixties that I became a feminist.

But then I met a very charming man and fell in love. Despite being halfway through law and much to my father's disappointment, I chucked in law and got married.

So, this is my timeline from that point:

Married at 21

Mother at 23

Sole parent at 24.

My father had just died, and my baby daughter and I moved to the NSW/Queensland border to live with my mother.

Sole parenting in the early seventies was far from easy. You dealt with the stigma of being a divorcee, being designated as a deserted wife, (great for the self-esteem) and the total lack of resources for childcare. I obtained work with solicitors in Coolangatta. One third of my gross pay went to babysitting fees. Again, I entered a male dominated profession and had to struggle to keep up with the boys. With apologies to any Queenslanders in the congregation, I loathed the Gold Coast, where frankly everyone was on the make, and when my daughter was five, I moved to Nowra on the south coast to be near my sister. I would live there for the next 45 years.

A couple of years after I moved, I had eye surgery for a congenital condition. And here is where my story starts to collide with Paul of Tarsus. Something went wrong with that surgery, and I came out with no sight. I was blind or close to blind for the next 6 months. I struggled with the thought of being disabled and unemployable for the rest of my life. I had a daughter to support. With very patient employers and remedial surgery I regained my sight and kept my job.

At this point in time my life felt like a complete failure – didn't finish law which had been my dream, caused my parents heaps of grief, broken marriage at 24 and recovering from the trauma of the botched surgery. – hardly the way we see our lives panning out. Working, running a home and being a mother guaranteed that

I probably didn't do any of them very well. Frankly, I didn't like myself or where my life was heading.

About this time after scrimping and saving, I bought myself a little cottage in the heart of Nowra. And my next-door neighbour was my Ananias. She befriended me and told me about Jesus. How simple it sounds "she told me about Jesus." How hard is it to tell someone about Jesus? To tell someone you hardly know. Ananias was courageous but so was my neighbour. A lot later I found out that many people at her church were praying for this encounter. How thankful we can be for faithful prayers. Eventually I said to my neighbour "How do I become a Christian" and she gave me a little booklet called "Four Spiritual Laws." I'm sure some of you will cringe at the mention of this booklet but it was my lifesaver.

So, what does this booklet say:

> God loves you and has a plan for your life.
>
> Jesus Christ is the way to God.
>
> Confess your sins and accept Jesus into your life.
>
> Live a life that reflects your faith.

On a cold winter's night on the 3rd of July 1980, I followed four spiritual laws and made my commitment to Jesus Christ. My whole life changed forever. Firstly, I experienced a beautiful spiritual high which lasted for about a week. This was an affirmation that I think Jesus knew I would need. Like Paul I needed a spectacular encounter.

But then reality stepped in, and I came down from that mountain and I knew I had to take practical steps. This was incredibly daunting. Firstly, I told my family who were at best nominal Christians. They were very kind. Susie has had a rotten time – this is a phase – she will get over it.

Then Oh help, I had to go to church – a place I had not seriously entered since my marriage. Do those who grow up in church realise what a cultural shock church can be for the unchurched? A gorgeous elderly lady at the door welcomed me with a beautiful smile. A shout out now to all the TUC welcomers. Without Stella's smile I may not have got across the threshold. The old Methodist church smelled musty, the pews were incredibly uncomfortable, and the music was classical. I was a rock and roll girl.

Nowra Uniting in its wisdom gave me two wonderful elders – people who encouraged me, accepted me, and set me on the path of reading my bible every day, something I still do. And again, I acknowledge the generosity of TUC in giving me a faithful pastoral carer as soon as I arrived.

Not long after I joined Nowra Uniting, the Superintendent of the Sunday School asked for volunteers to teach. My daughter was reluctant to go to Sunday School so I thought I can do this. The Superintendent instead of saying "You are too new a Christian", accepted me. This was despite less than unanimous support from the eldership, as I found out later. The Superintendent, in her wisdom gave me a mentor and we taught together. I loved teaching children and some years later I would become Superintendent myself. I went on to work with children in KUCA (Kids of the Uniting Church of Australia), scripture in schools and then youth and young adults. Later I would go on to achieve my Lay Preachers accreditation. I loved it all. But at that early stage, I could have walked away- my faith was fragile. It was love and acceptance that kept me there.

The following year after my conversion, I decided I wanted to be baptised in the Shoalhaven River. Jesus was baptised so that's what I wanted. Now as I have told you I was christened in the Anglican church and the Uniting church decrees one baptism. I didn't know that so how brave was my minister at the time to decide that my spiritual journey warranted him breaking the rules. Somehow, I don't think Jesus would have condemned him. I think that we have courageous ministers, one who doesn't mind when you disagree with her as I am wont to do on occasions. I am hard work.

What I was gradually learning on my faith journey was that Christianity is not first and foremost a religion; it is a relationship. Like Paul, I had to break away from my old life, deal with the challenges and hang on, sometimes by my fingernails, to Jesus. I have not suffered like Paul, been flogged, imprisoned or shipwrecked (well not yet anyway) but I have had my challenges. The love of Christ that accepted me, forgave me, and befriended me has kept me going for the last 45 years.

There were phases of this journey,

Evangelical – learning the stories, reading my bible, sharing my faith, getting involved with the church.

Charismatic – not just about waving your hands in the air which I do with enthusiasm but leaning about the gifts of the spirit and using them for the building up of the body of Christ.

Contemplative when I learned the Mary thing which Andi spoke so beautifully about recently – sitting at the feet of Jesus – learning to be the Beloved. Seeing the depth of intimacy that Jesus offers to us and calls us into.

And then my more liberal phase – disposing of some of my hangups, inappropriate prejudices and judgmentalism.

I am grateful for all of that. All enabled me to see Jesus in a different light.

And now I am into my older age. I look forward to spending eternity with Jesus but not just yet – there is still life in the old dog! But in these years, I long to say as Paul did "I want to know Christ and the power of his resurrection." To know the infilling of the Holy Spirit to grow the fruit of the Spirit. I want somehow to reflect the incredible love and sacrifice that took Jesus to the cross and set my whole life on a different path.

For that love and sacrifice I am and always will be eternally grateful.

20

AROUND ABOUT

A Vision to work with Indigenous Peoples

I grew up on a sheep and wheat farm in the Riverina in the 1950s and 1960s. Our closest little town where we attended Mass each Sunday was 20km away. Even though I had two sisters, eight and six years older and a brother four years older, my childhood was not a lonely, but an alone experience.

We were raised Catholic by a mother who was faithful to her religion all her life and who at age 83 died peacefully with her rosary beads in her hands. My father gave up attending church when I was six or so. We travelled an hour each way on the school bus to the convent school in the nearest big town. Some of the nuns were caring gentle women and I stayed in contact with my Year 6 teacher till she died a few years ago.

As soon as I finished Year 12, I moved to Sydney to work, met my husband, also Catholic, and had one daughter in Sydney then our second daughter in Canberra three years later where we had moved to for my husband's work. We were both regular church goers and brought our daughters up in the faith and sent them to Catholic schools.

We divorced after seventeen years of marriage. At this stage I became more involved in my local church and made good friends who supported me through the difficult times.

In 1995 I was holidaying in the Northern Territory with a couple from my church and we attended Sunday Mass in Alice Springs. The Gospel reading from Luke 10 was the story of Martha and Mary. As a worker, like Martha, I was reflecting on the sermon where the priest gave a more sympathetic interpretation of her compared with Mary who chose the better path. Apparently, I went into a deep meditative state as I was unaware of a disturbance behind us when someone had a medical incident and the ambulance was called. During this time, I believe I heard Jesus say to me "I want you to work with my people." And I had a vision of Indigenous people.

We returned to Canberra at the end of our holiday and I set about finding work with Indigenous people. Six months later, having taken two years leave without pay from my public service position, I began working as a volunteer house mother caring for eight Indigenous girls aged 13-14 years in a boarding hostel on a 32,000 acre sheep and wheat station at Tardun, 150km east of Geraldton, WA. The station had originally been established to provide an income to facilitate the work of the Pallottine Fathers and Brothers working with Indigenous people in the Kimberley, including Balgo Community. At the request of Indigenous people working on stations around Tardun the Pallottines began a boarding hostel and school to educate their children during school terms and the children returned to their families for holidays. To say this was an interesting time is an understatement!

While there I met the man who became my second husband. He also was working as a volunteer driving the high school students to Morawa District High School, 70km from the hostel. After two years at Tardun, we volunteered to work as house parents with two Christian Brothers in a respite home for troubled teenage boys in Townsville. Sadly, the home closed at the end of our first year as the Order couldn't find replacements for the two Brothers who were worn out after many years working with these boys.

In our next "posting" I did the administrative work for the Mercy Community Health Service which was being handed over to Indigenous management. We were located in the remote community of Balgo on the edge of the Tanami Desert, 120km south of Halls Creek, WA. As well as Balgo we managed health clinics in the surrounding remote communities of Billiluna, Mulan and Yagga Yagga. The remote area nurses were marvellous, but

Indigenous health in remote areas is problematic. During that year my husband provided literacy support in the Catholic school.

When this finished, we volunteered for another year as houseparents to the senior high school boys at the boarding hostel at Tardun.

You did not choose me, but I chose you and appointed you to go and bear fruit - fruit that will last, (John 15:16) was the quote that sustained me during this five year period of volunteering.

We returned to Canberra to find paid work (I'd had to resign from the Public Service), but I had the bright (but dumb) idea that I'd retrain as a primary school teacher at the Australian Catholic university. My first teaching appointment was at the Catholic Primary School in Brewarrina.

My next position was at the Catholic school which was co-located with the boarding hostel at Tardun. This was a great experience and I enjoyed seeing my Year 1-3 students progress as they attended school each day and had supportive houseparents who listened to them read each night. My husband was driving the school bus again and doing other work as a volunteer around the hostel. However, it was not to be. Once again we were jobless and homeless when the school abruptly closed at the end of the year.

We bought a small farm near Eugowra and busily planted hundreds of trees to revegetate it, became involved in the local community and local Catholic Church. After two years farming, my husband became restless to work again with Indigenous people and I found a position in the Catholic School in Billiluna In the Kimberley, near Balgo. Again I enjoyed teaching Year 6-7 students in my first year and K-Year 2 students in my second year.

The Catholic faith was strong in both Balgo and Billiluna and living in both communities was an enriching experience culturally and spiritually.

We returned to the farm for another Seven years, interrupted by a six month teaching stint at the Catholic High School in Nguiu on

Bathurst Island, 70km north of Darwin. At the end of 2014 we sold the farm as we both had health issues and moved to Canberra to retire. Unfortunately our marriage didn't survive and my husband moved to Brisbane to be near his family.

On return to Canberra, I attended the Catholic Church in Kambah, but never connected with it. I became progressively more disillusioned with the Catholic Church generally and finally ceased attending. However, my Catholic upbringing was too strong and it didn't feel right not to be part of a church. After a few months, I moved to the Anglican Church at Pearce which was more welcoming, but despite strong involvement for several years I found it too conservative for me. I finally feel that I have found my home at Tuggeranong Uniting Church.

As I've aged, I've found that my spirituality has matured and my mantra now is *Love one another. As I have loved you, so you must love one another.* (John13:34)

www.ingramcontent.com/pod-product-compliance
Ingram Content Group UK Ltd.
Pitfield, Milton Keynes, MK11 3LW, UK
UKHW062256290726
14090UKWH00017B/717